Child Sexual Abuse

Other books in the At Issue series:

Anorexia
Antidepressants
Anti-Semitism
Are Chain Stores Ruining America?
Are Privacy Rights Being Violated?
Attention Deficit/Hyperactivity Disorder
Biological and Chemical Weapons
Child Labor and Sweatshops
Cosmetic Surgery
Creationism Versus Evolution
Do Children Have Rights?
Does Advertising Promote Substance Abuse?
Does the Internet Benefit Society?
Does the Internet Increase the Risk of Crime?
Does the United States Need a National Health Insurance
    Policy?
Drugs and Sports
The Ethics of Abortion
The Future of the Internet
How Can the Poor Be Helped?
How Should One Cope with Death?
How Should Prisons Treat Inmates?
How Should Society Address the Needs of the Elderly?
How Should the United States Treat Prisoners in the War on
    Terror?
Indian Gaming
Is American Culture in Decline?
Is Islam a Religion of War or Peace?
Is It Unpatriotic to Criticize One's Country?
Islam in America
Is Poverty a Serious Problem?
Is the Gap Between the Rich and Poor Growing?
Is There Life After Death?
Is the World Heading Toward an Energy Crisis?
Is Torture Ever Justified?
Legalizing Drugs
Managing America's Forests
Nuclear and Toxic Waste
Protecting America's Borders
Religion and Education
Space Exploration
Teen Sex
What Are the Most Serious Threats to National Security?
What Causes Addiction?
What Is the State of Human Rights?
Women in Islam

At ✳ Issue

Child Sexual Abuse

Angela Lewis, *Book Editor*

Bruce Glassman, *Vice President*
Bonnie Szumski, *Publisher*
Helen Cothran, *Managing Editor*

GREENHAVEN PRESS
An imprint of Thomson Gale, a part of The Thomson Corporation

THOMSON

GALE

Detroit • New York • San Francisco • San Diego • New Haven, Conn.
Waterville, Maine • London • Munich

For more information, contact
Greenhaven Press
27500 Drake Rd.
Farmington Hills, MI 48331-3535
Or you can visit our Internet site at http://www.gale.com

LIBRARY OF CONGRESS CATALOGING-IN-PUBLICATION DATA
Child sexual abuse / Angela Lewis, book editor.
p. cm. — (At issue)
Includes bibliographical references and index.
ISBN 0-7377-2363-7 (pbk. : alk. paper) —
ISBN 0-7377-2362-9 (lib. bdg. : alk. paper)
1. Child sexual abuse—United States. I. Lewis, Angela. II. At issue (San Diego, Calif.)
HV6570.2.C45 2005
362.276'0973—dc22   2004059683

Contents

Page

Introduction   7

1. Child Sexual Abuse Has Declined   11
   David Finkelhor and Lisa M. Jones

2. Child Sexual Abuse in Schools Is a Serious Problem   17
   Caroline Hendrie

3. The Scope and Nature of Child Sexual Abuse in the   23
   Catholic Church
   *National Review Board for the Protection of Children and
   Young People*

4. Law Enforcement Efforts Against Child Pornography   35
   Are Ineffective
   Philip Jenkins

5. Law Enforcement Efforts Against Child Pornography   41
   Are Effective
   John Ashcroft et al.

6. Child Prostitution Laws Victimize Children   50
   Joan Ryan

7. Panic over Child Sexual Abuse Has Led to Unjust   54
   Civil Commitment Laws
   Mark McHarry

8. Satellite Tracking of Sex Offenders May Be More   64
   Effective than Civil Commitment
   Lori Montgomery and Daniel LeDuc

9. Sex Offender Registration Laws Protect Children   69
   David Tell

10. Pedophilia Is Linked to Homosexuality   77
    Timothy J. Dailey

11. Pedophilia Is Not Linked to Homosexuality   86
    Gregory M. Herek

12. Child Sexual Abuse by Females Is a Growing Problem   96
   Maura Dolan

13. Pedophiles Use the Internet to Find Victims   104
   Peter Wilkinson

Organizations to Contact   111

Bibliography   117

Index   120

Introduction

Megan Nicole Kanka was only seven years old when her neighbor Jesse Timmendequas lured her into his house with the promise of seeing a puppy. On July 29, 1994, the twice-convicted sex offender then sexually assaulted, beat, and strangled Megan to death with a belt.

The nation was outraged that a convicted sex offender had been released from prison with no warning to the Hamilton, New Jersey, community. According to the Megan Nicole Kanka Foundation, Megan's parents immediately began lobbying for legislation to ensure that, "at the very least, any convicted pedophile released from prison can not be allowed to reside in neighborhoods without the knowledge of parents and children in that neighborhood."

The Kankas' efforts were successful, and on May 17, 1996, President Clinton signed Megan's Law, which requires states to create sex offender registry and notification systems. Under this federal law, states collect the names, addresses, fingerprints, and photographs of offenders, along with descriptions of the crimes committed. The information is then listed on a registry that is available to the public.

The intention of Megan's Law is to ensure the safety of children, but there has been an ongoing debate about its constitutionality. At issue are the offenders' right to privacy, due process, the right not to be punished after completing the sentence for a crime (ex post facto), and the right not to suffer cruel and unusual punishment.

Sex offenders argue that their right to privacy is violated when states provide the public with their detailed personal information. Offenders assert that by distributing their names and addresses, states are not affording them the privacy they need to successfully reenter society. Sex offenders argue that broad notification methods, such as Internet registries, deny them even the smallest opportunity to begin anew after their release.

Advocates of Megan's Law believe that public safety outweighs a sex offender's right to privacy. They assert that only properly informed parents are able to protect their children.

Richard Kanka best expressed this sentiment when he stated, "If we had been aware of his [Timmendequas's] record, my daughter would be alive today."

Sex offenders have also argued that Megan's Law denies them their constitutional right to due process, or the right to full and fair court proceedings. For example, in the 2003 case of *Connecticut Department of Public Safety v. Doe*, a convicted sex offender (Doe) challenged the state's authority to list him on a sex offender registry without first providing him the opportunity to prove that he was no longer dangerous. Doe argued that because he was denied an evaluation to assess his level of dangerousness, he was denied his right to due process. By placing his name on the registry without this evaluation, Doe argued, the state defamed him and stigmatized him with the label "sex offender."

Connecticut attorney general Richard Blumenthal spoke for proponents of Megan's Law when he argued that all convicted sex offenders have been afforded due process through the initial criminal proceedings. He stated, "Every person on the registry has been convicted of an offense that is extraordinarily serious after a full and fair proceeding." In response to the claim that Doe had been stigmatized with an unwarranted label, Blumenthal replied, "The stigma was created by the sex offender who committed the crime and it is in no way defamatory or branding because it is simply truthful, accurate information."

The U.S. Supreme Court was convinced by Blumenthal and upheld Connecticut's sex offender registry law. The Court held that an individual evaluation of offenders was not necessary and that Connecticut could continue to require all convicted sex offenders to register. In the opinion of the Court, due process had been granted during the original criminal proceeding.

Another criticism of Megan's Law is that it punishes sex offenders ex post facto. The use of the Internet for distribution of registry information is of particular concern. Sex offender advocates assert that the worldwide distribution of registration information impedes a released offender's reentry into society. They claim that released offenders are often ostracized or harassed and insist that these consequences of Megan's Law, even if unintended, constitute continued punishment.

Some sex offender advocates take this argument a step further and argue that offenders experience such hardship as a result of the law, that it constitutes not only continued punishment but also cruel and unusual punishment. In his article

"Revisiting Megan's Law and Sex Offender Registration: Prevention or Problem," child sexual abuse prevention expert Robert E. Longo cites examples of offenders who have been excluded from employment and housing. He asks, "When these laws harm sex offenders and others, such as families and other community members, beyond the intent of the law, how can one not consider the impact as cruel, unusual, and excessive punishment?"

Proponents of the use of Internet registries and Megan's Law insist that the intent of the law is not to punish offenders. Rather, it is to increase public awareness and ensure the safety of children. On March 5, 2003, in *Smith v. Doe*, the U.S. Supreme Court upheld this opinion and concluded that posting registry information on the Internet is not continued punishment of the offender. Again, the concern for public safety was established as a priority over the individual rights of the offender.

In addition to being concerned about the violation of constitutional rights, critics believe that Megan's Law inadvertently undermines public safety. A frequent assertion is that sex offender registration and community notification lull the public into a false sense of security. Critics cite research findings showing that 88 percent of child sexual abuse is never reported, only 3 percent of offenders are convicted, and only a percentage of those are listed on sex offender registries. Therefore, considering community notification as a catchall solution that adequately warns communities about the presence of sex offenders is unrealistic at best, and dangerous at worst.

Critics also point out that in most cases of child sexual abuse, the perpetrator is not a stranger but someone the child knows. Alisa Klein is the director of Stop It Now, a nonprofit organization that encourages abusers to seek help. She states,

> If we're promoting this myth that sexual offenders are these horrible scary monsters, people are never going to be able to face the fact that we have sexual abusers in our families, among our friends— people that we know and love and trust.

Proponents of community notification do not deny that the majority of victims of child sexual abuse know their perpetrators. However, they do not agree that Megan's Law lulls the public into a false sense of security. Rather, they argue that community notification provides a unique opportunity for raising public awareness about child sexual abuse. Advocates support the use of community meetings for the dual purpose of notification and providing residents with accurate information about sex offenders and the problem of child sexual abuse.

Indeed, increased public awareness regarding child sexual abuse has proven to be a positive result of Megan's Law. As part of an evaluation of Washington State's Community Protection Act, a survey was conducted to solicit public opinion regarding community notification laws. One of the most salient findings was that nearly 75 percent of the respondents said that they had learned more about sex offenders and the nature of child sexual abuse because of community notification.

The discussion regarding the constitutionality and effectiveness of Megan's Law is sure to continue. However, the issue of sex offender registration and community notification is only one of the many debates about child sexual abuse. The authors in this anthology discuss other related topics with the goal of raising awareness about one of the most taboo subjects in society—the sexual abuse of children.

1

Child Sexual Abuse Has Declined

David Finkelhor and Lisa M. Jones

David Finkelhor is a professor of sociology and the director of the Crimes Against Children Research Center at the University of New Hampshire. Lisa M. Jones is a research assistant professor of psychology at the same center.

Between 1992 and 2000, the number of substantiated cases of child sexual abuse declined by 40 percent. The decline may be partially due to decreased reporting and changes in the procedures used by child protective services (CPS) agencies. However, there is strong evidence that a real decline in child sexual abuse occurred. For example, the number of self-reports of sexual abuse by victims has decreased. Also, many other indicators of crime and family problems declined during the same period, suggesting a general improvement in the well-being of children. Large-scale prevention and intervention efforts may be contributing to the decline.

The number of sexual abuse cases substantiated by child protective service (CPS) agencies dropped a remarkable 40 percent between 1992 and 2000, from an estimated 150,000 cases to 89,500 cases, but professional opinion is divided about why. It is possible that the incidence of sexual abuse has declined as a result of two decades of prevention, treatment, and aggressive criminal justice activity. It is also possible that there has been no real decline, and that the apparent decline is explained by a drop in the number of cases being identified and reported or by

David Finkelhor and Lisa M. Jones, "Explanations for the Decline in Child Sexual Abuse Cases," *Juvenile Justice Bulletin*, 2004.

changes in practices of child protection agencies. Identifying the source or sources of the decline in the number of substantiated sexual abuse cases is important. The possibility that a real decline occurred is heartening and could point the way to more effective strategies for preventing all kinds of child maltreatment. On the other hand, if the decline is due solely to decreased reporting or changes in CPS procedures, it could mean that more children are failing to get the help and services they need. . . .

Key Findings

- Detailed data provided by four state CPS agencies offered little evidence that the decline was due either to more conservative judgment by CPS about the types of sexual abuse cases they would investigate or substantiate or to increasing reluctance by CPS to become involved in cases in which the perpetrator is not a primary caregiver.
- There also was no strong evidence that the decline was largely due to a diminishing reservoir of older, ongoing cases available for new disclosures.
- There was some evidence that the sexual abuse decline in one state could be partly explained by changes in CPS procedures and data collection methods. According to national data, however, this explanation does not successfully account for the declines seen in the majority of states.
- There was mixed evidence that reporting of sexual abuse to CPS declined because of a "backlash," that is, a greater public and professional skepticism about reports of sexual abuse.
- Evidence from a number of different sources, including National Crime Victimization Survey (NCVS) data showing a 56-percent decline in self-reported sexual assault against juveniles, is consistent with a real decline in sexual abuse.
- Finally, additional studies and improved data are needed to make crucially important decisions for public policy based on the factors that are most responsible for the decline. . . .

Evidence of a True Decline

No solid and convincing explanation exists for why sexual abuse cases declined in the 1990s, although it is important to try to find out why a decline occurred. The answer, if it can be determined, is not likely to be a simple one. In all likelihood, multiple factors were involved in the trend. Based on the strength of current evidence, one of those factors was probably a true decline in the occurrence of sexual abuse. Changes in the practices of professionals who report suspected abuse and of the child protective system probably also have played a part, but how large a part is difficult to ascertain.

The evidence for some true decline in incidents of sexual abuse comes from several directions. One is the decline in self-report measures of sexual assault and sexual abuse. The NCVS and the Minnesota Student Survey are both crucial indicators that are independent of the filtering or policies of social agencies. Although validity problems are always present with the self-reporting of sensitive information, there are no strong reasons to think that candor about sexual abuse has declined.

The number of sexual abuse cases substantiated by child protective service (CPS) agencies dropped a remarkable 40 percent between 1992 and 2000.

Another strong piece of evidence for a true decline is the improvement in many other indicators of crime, sexual behavior, and family problems over the same period of time. The decline in these areas suggests general movement toward improvement in the well-being of children. An actual decline in the number of sexual abuse cases seems more plausible in the context of such a trend than it would if the other factors had not improved.

More attention has been focused on child sexual abuse during the past two decades [1980–2000] than on any other form of child maltreatment. It should not be surprising that its decline would come before and be greater than that of other forms of maltreatment. Prevention and intervention efforts have included school-based prevention education, treatment programs for juvenile and adult offenders, and greatly enhanced resources for criminal justice investigation and prosecution. It is reasonable to think that, given the scale of these efforts, they have had some success in preventing or intervening in sexual abuse.

The relatively inconsistent evidence for other explanations of the decline in the number of sexual abuse cases also supports the possibility of a true decline in sexual abuses. . . . The other explanations do not lack evidence. Indeed, some states clearly have made statistical and administrative changes that have contributed to the decline. There is evidence both that allegations involving very young children have declined more, perhaps because such cases have less credibility, and that cases involving young perpetrators may have declined because they are seen as outside the purview of the child protection system. Evidence from at least one state is consistent with the possibility that some of the decline in substantiated cases of sexual abuse may be due to a backlash against those who report it.

Taken together, however, the evidence for these other explanations seems to exist only in some places or to explain only a small portion of the decline in substantiated cases. The decline has been so widespread geographically and has occurred across so many categories of children, offenders, types of abuse, and types of evidence that a true decline can be considered as at least one part of the overall picture.

Concerns About Future Funding

Many observers of the decline in the number of substantiated sexual abuse cases, including state officials, have seemed resistant to the possibility that the numbers represent a true decline, preferring almost any other explanation as an alternative. This attitude may stem from a concern that if people believe sexual abuse is waning, their vigilance and concern about the problem and willingness to support funding will disappear. Increasing numbers of cases were part of what mobilized people and resources during the 1980s, so declining numbers of cases might have the opposite effect.

Although social problems go through a well-recognized issue/attention cycle and some changes have occurred in the media attitude toward sexual abuse, there are reasons to doubt that a true decline in incidence of the current magnitude could, if recognized, result in a massive desertion of interest or funding. For one, the public and professional interest in the issue of sexual abuse has roots that go far beyond the matter of whether it involves 50,000 or 150,000 cases per year, and relate to the now well-established role that it plays in discussions of family problems, gender relations, sexuality, and mental health. The high-profile public and professional role this problem has achieved in recent years will not easily change. Second, the other social problems discussed above that also have experienced recent declines do not appear to have suffered any social policy desertion as a result. Homicide, crime, and teen pregnancy are all still issues of ongoing serious policy attention, despite their declines, because they remain serious problems even at reduced levels. The declines may, in fact, have spurred policy interest because problems that fester for a long time without improvement in spite of considerable policy attention become frustrating. Policymakers and the public can become discouraged and decide that such problems are beyond immediate solution. Signs of success from social initiatives can provide the public and policymakers with energy and justification for expanded efforts to reinforce what appears to be working. Of course, the factors influencing public interest and policymaking are complex, but there is no strong reason to believe that evidence of a true decline in sexual abuse by itself will have negative effects on the policy environment around the problem.

The Need to Identify Reasons for Decline

Because social policy benefits from understanding the factors that result in success, the hypothesis that sexual abuse has declined should be accepted, and identifying the reasons why it has declined should be a priority. It is extremely important that lessons be drawn from a change of this magnitude in a social problem that has been considered so widespread and corrosive to the well-being of children, families, and communities. Several initiatives might be considered to deepen our understanding.

> *Many observers . . . have seemed resistant to the possibility that the numbers represent a true decline, preferring almost any other explanation as an alternative.*

First, more intensive studies need to be undertaken in individual localities where a full inventory of explanations could be considered, with both quantitative and qualitative evidence available. In individual localities, it may be easier to observe how policy and programmatic changes, including prosecution initiatives, treatment resources, and educational programs, may have been sequenced with the onset or acceleration of a decline in sexual abuse. In addition, localities with different trend patterns (steady declines, increases, no change, and fluctuating patterns) should be compared with one another, and it might be useful if such localities were in the same state and were comparable in other ways. Some local studies might center around the case records of investigative agencies that have maintained stable policies, catchment areas, and detailed recordkeeping practices over a long period, from which it might be ascertained more accurately how case characteristics have changed over time.

It would also greatly help the analysis of the current decline and future trends if data systems relating to relevant factors would be expanded, enhanced, and improved. Currently, data on sex crimes against children are artificially divided between the child protective system and the law enforcement system in a way that prohibits a comprehensive assessment of trends in the whole problem. Data from state child protection systems are not gathered in ways that are comparable across jurisdictions; therefore, comparisons of the effects of different policy environments are difficult. In the justice area, systematic information is not readily available on the demographics of persons prosecuted, convicted, incarcerated, or treated for sex crimes against children.

In addition, an understanding of the reasons for the decline has been greatly hampered by the failure of communities to evaluate their varied prevention and intervention efforts. More effort should be made prospectively to observe trends and outcomes as communities implement various prosecution, treatment, community, and school-based educational efforts. In this way, a better inventory of the more and less successful strategies could be tracked in conjunction with the relative decline in different locales.

Researchers may not be able to fully answer the question of why this most recent decline has occurred; however, it is important to be better prepared to understand the sources of any continuing or future declines. To what extent do prevention education, increased public awareness, greater prosecution, and incarceration play roles? Answering such questions can help policymakers formulate policies that will extend and accelerate the decline in sexual abuse and, perhaps, in other forms of child maltreatment.

Child Sexual Abuse in Schools Is a Serious Problem

Caroline Hendrie

Caroline Hendrie is a senior editor for Education Week.

A report commissioned by the U.S. Department of Education found that thousands of students experience some kind of sexual abuse by public school employees every year. The report also noted that students are much more likely to experience sexual abuse at school than to be sexually mistreated by priests or deacons in the Catholic Church—an institution that has been shaken by many reports of abuse in recent years. More research into the pervasiveness of sexual abuse in schools is needed. However, the education community should not wait for further data before taking action to prevent abuse.

A draft report commissioned by the U.S. Department of Education concludes that far too little is known about the prevalence of sexual misconduct by teachers or other school employees, but estimates that millions of children are being affected by it during their school-age years.

Written in response to a requirement in the federal No Child Left Behind Act, the report by a university-based expert on schoolhouse sexual misconduct concludes that the issue "is woefully understudied" and that solid national data on its prevalence are sorely needed.

Yet despite the limitations of the existing research base, the

Caroline Hendrie, "Sexual Abuse by Educators Is Scrutinized," *Education Week*, vol. 23, March 10, 2004, pp. 1, 16. Reproduced by permission.

scope of the problem appears to far exceed the priest abuse scandal in the Roman Catholic Church, said Charol Shakeshaft, the Hofstra University scholar who prepared the report.

The best data available suggest that nearly 10 percent of American students are targets of unwanted sexual attention by public school employees—ranging from sexual comments to rape—at some point during their school-age years, Ms. Shakeshaft said.

"So we think the Catholic Church has a problem?" she said.

To support her contention that many more youngsters have been sexually mistreated by school employees than by priests, Ms. Shakeshaft pointed to research conducted for the U.S. Conference of Catholic Bishops and released late last month [February 2004]. That study found that from 1950 to 2002, 10,667 people made allegations that priests or deacons had sexually abused them as minors.

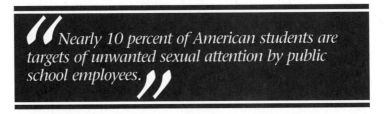

Nearly 10 percent of American students are targets of unwanted sexual attention by public school employees.

Extrapolating from data collected in a national survey for the American Association of University Women Educational Foundation in 2000, Ms. Shakeshaft estimated that roughly 290,000 students experienced some sort of physical sexual abuse by a public school employee from 1991 to 2000—a single decade, compared with the roughly five-decade period examined in the study of Catholic priests.

Those figures suggest that "the physical sexual abuse of students in schools is likely more than 100 times the abuse by priests," contended Ms. Shakeshaft, who is a professor of educational administration at Hofstra, in Hempstead, N.Y.

Kathleen Lyons, a spokeswoman for the National Education Association, called it "a misuse of the data to imply that public schools and the Catholic Church have experienced the same level of abuse cases."

"I take great umbrage at that suggestion," she said in an interview. "That just seems like someone is reaching conclusions based on half the data that's needed."

Ms. Shakeshaft acknowledged that the accuracy of such

comparisons might be thrown off by any number of factors, including undercounting of youngsters abused by priests. But that uncertainty only underscores the need for better research on the prevalence of sexual misconduct in the schools, she argued.

"Educator sexual misconduct is woefully understudied," Ms. Shakeshaft says in the draft of her report, titled "Educator Sexual Misconduct: A Synthesis of Existing Literature."

"We have scant data on incidence and even less on descriptions of predators and targets," she writes. "There are many questions that call for answers."

Law Required Study

The Education Department contracted with Ms. Shakeshaft to examine what is known about the prevalence of sexual misconduct against students by school employees. The agency was responding to a provision in the No Child Left Behind Act.

The little-noticed provision required a "study regarding the prevalence of sexual abuse in schools, including recommendations and legislative remedies for addressing the problem of sexual abuse in schools." The provision went on to set a completion date of "not later than 18 months" after the enactment of the law, which was signed by President Bush in January 2002.

Ms. Shakeshaft said her initial understanding from the department was that she was to conduct a review of the existing research to set the stage for a broad national study. She said the department had interpreted the statute's reference to "sexual abuse in schools" as meaning misconduct by school employees against students, and not by students against their peers.

The physical sexual abuse of students in school is likely more than 100 times the abuse by priests.

She said that after she turned in a draft of the report last May [2003], she received feedback from the department that led her to believe that the literature review was no longer intended to lay the groundwork for a future study. In a letter stating that the Education Department "has not made plans to conduct further work on a national study on sexual abuse in schools," Ms. Shakeshaft was asked to change the original subtitle of her report, which was "A Synthesis of Existing Literature in Connection With the Design of a National Analysis."

Ms. Shakeshaft then retooled and expanded the report to include more information about what is known about the issue, and submitted another draft to the department last week [March 2004].

Carlin Mertz, an Education Department spokesman, said . . . that officials did not want to make substantive comments about the report until it had been reviewed by the agency and made final. But he indicated that the department did not intend a full-blown study of the issue at the present time.

"That's all we're going to do right now," said Mr. Mertz. "Right now, this is it."

If no additional study is commissioned, Ms. Shakeshaft will be disappointed, she said.

"A review of what we know about educator sexual misconduct tells us that in order to prevent incidents, we really need to know more about it," she said.

Leadership at the federal level is needed, she argued, because of the decentralization of the U.S. education system.

"There's no one school district for the whole country," she said. "The only place we can go really to do a national study is the federal government."

Gregory Lawler, a lawyer for the Colorado Education Association who co-wrote a book published [in 2003] titled *Guilty Until Proven Innocent: Teachers and Accusations of Abuse*, said last week [March 2004] that he agreed that better data were needed at a national level.

"National Education Association, or somebody, ought to be keeping records of both sex- and child-abuse allegations and where they go," Mr. Lawler said. "There should be a database somewhere, because I think it would help put things in context."

Data Flawed

In her report, Ms. Shakeshaft identifies nearly 900 citations in research-based sources—described as "all sources that were screened for an empirical or systematic analytic foundation"—"that discussed educator sexual misconduct in some format."

But of those, she found just 14 empirical studies on the subject from the United States, Canada, or the United Kingdom.

Two of those were conducted by *Education Week* and were chronicled in separate series of articles published in 1998 and 2003. ("A Trust Betrayed: Sexual Abuse by Teachers" November 1998, and "A Trust Betrayed: Update on Sexual Misconduct in Schools," April 2003.)

"None of these studies—either singly or as a group—answer all of the reasonable questions that parents, students, educators, and the public ask about educator sexual misconduct," Ms. Shakeshaft says in the draft report. "And they certainly do not provide information at a level of reliability and validity appropriate to the gravity of these offenses."

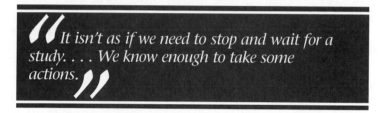

It isn't as if we need to stop and wait for a study. . . . We know enough to take some actions.

Of the data available, Ms. Shakeshaft views a 2001 study by the American Association of University Women (AAUW) as offering the best window into how many schoolchildren are targets of sexual misconduct by educators.

Based on a 2000 survey of 2,064 public school students in grades 8–11, "Hostile Hallways II: Bullying, Teasing, and Sexual Harassment in School" was a follow-up to a similar study the Washington-based AAUW conducted in 1993.

While the AAUW studies did not focus on misconduct by school employees, both of the surveys featured questions about sexual harassment that Ms. Shakeshaft was able to reanalyze for information on the prevalence of such behavior.

The reanalysis found that 9.6 percent of all students in grades 8–11 reported sexual harassment by teachers, coaches, or other school employees. That included misconduct involving physical contact as well as such behavior as sexual remarks, jokes, or gestures, with 8.7 percent of respondents reporting "noncontact" harassment and 6.7 percent reporting harassment involving physical contact.

A Need for Further Study

While Ms. Shakeshaft considers the AAUW data the best available for estimating the prevalence of the problem, the information has many limitations, she notes in her report. Among them are that the survey asked students to "report on their entire school career, making it difficult to determine prevalence by year or grade" and increasing the likelihood that students might have forgotten about incidents in earlier years.

"Analysis was broad-brushed and cursory," Ms. Shakeshaft adds in the draft report, and "questions on educator sexual misconduct are limited." Moreover, inappropriate behavior by educators was likely underreported, she suggests, because the survey "only asked about incidents that were unwanted, excluding reports of misconduct that were either welcome or that did not fall into either a welcome or unwelcome category."

Still, she says in the report that the data can be used to "get a sense of the extent of the number of students who have been targets of educator sexual misconduct."

"Based on the assumption that the AAUW surveys accurately represent the experiences of all K–12 students, more than 4.5 million students are sexually harassed or abused by an employee of a school sometime between kindergarten and 12th grade," the report says. "This is about the same number of people who live in all of Alaska, Delaware, Montana, North Dakota, South Dakota, Vermont, and Wyoming."

To help fill the holes in the knowledge base on schoolhouse sexual misconduct, Ms. Shakeshaft recommends further research on topics including prevalence and patterns of abuse, effects on targets and other students, consequences for offenders, and responses by schools, districts, professional organizations, and the public.

She also calls for study of effective investigative practices, the legal landscape, and state laws and policies. The frequency of false accusations is another area she cites as being worthy of examination.

But as strongly as she feels that more research is needed, Ms. Shakeshaft said the education community shouldn't sit on its hands.

"Some individual districts might have changed some policies or had an in-service workshop, but really there hasn't been any systematic response to this issue," she said. "It isn't as if we need to stop and wait for a study. I do believe we know enough to take some actions."

3

The Scope and Nature of Child Sexual Abuse in the Catholic Church

National Review Board for the Protection of Children and Young People

The National Review Board for the Protection of Children and Young People is a group of lay Catholics that includes lawyers, clinical counselors, education professionals, judges, psychiatrists, former congressional members, and other professionals. The review board was established by the United States Conference of Catholic Bishops to study the problem of sexual abuse by priests and deacons in the Catholic Church, to make recommendations on its findings, and to further advocate for victims of sexual abuse.

A study commissioned by the United Stated Conference of Catholic Bishops found that sexual abuse of minors by priests and deacons in the Catholic Church is a serious problem. The study highlighted the fact that 4 percent of priests who were in the ministry between 1950 and 2002 have been accused of abuse. These accusations were made mostly by male victims between the ages of eleven and seventeen. The U.S. Conference of Catholic Bishops acknowledges the fact that victims were treated unfairly. The bishops admit that in many cases the church's concern for the accused priests outweighed concern for the victims and that relatively few priests were reported to civil authorities. In retrospect, the bishops recognize that secrecy, avoidance of scandal, and misguided forgiveness of perpetrators have contributed

National Review Board for the Protection of Children and Young People, *The Nature and Scope of the Problem of Sexual Abuse of Minors by Catholic Priests and Deacons in the United States: A Research Study Conducted by the John Jay College of Criminal Justice*, March 3, 2003.

to continued abuse. The church now imposes a zero tolerance policy on sex offenders. No priest who commits sexual abuse will be allowed to continue in the ministry.

The [National Review Board for the Protection of Children and Young People] believes that the overwhelming majority of priests serving the Church in the United States fulfill their roles honorably and chastely. According to Church records, however, there were credible allegations that several thousand priests, comprising four percent of priests in ministry over the last half-century, committed acts of sexual abuse of minors. There appears to have been a significant surge in acts of abuse beginning in the 1960s and continuing into the mid-1980s. The fallout resulting from this epidemic of abuse and the shortcomings in the response of a number of bishops and other Church leaders to that misconduct continues to this day.

The crime of sexual abuse of minors is not a problem unique to the Catholic clergy. As Pope John Paul II stated prior to the adoption of the Charter [for the protection of Children and Young People], "Abuse of the young is a grave symptom of a crisis affecting not only the Church but society as a whole." Indeed, it is a contemporary societal problem that affects numerous families and many secular organizations as well as other churches and ecclesial communities. Although some evidence suggests that the abuse epidemic afflicted many institutions and organizations in our country, it is beyond the Board's mission to determine whether the problem was more pervasive among Catholic clergy than it was in other sectors of society or in the general population. Reliable statistical evidence of the sexual abuse of minors is particularly difficult to obtain because, according to experts, many if not most acts of abuse occur within families and often are not reported.

Bishops Take Responsibility

Nevertheless, the number of incidents of sexual abuse of minors by Catholic clergy, at least over the past fifty years, is significant and disturbing. This is a failing not simply on the part of the priests who sexually abused minors but also on the part of those bishops and other Church leaders who did not act effectively to preclude that abuse in the first instance or respond appropriately when it occurred. These leadership failings have been shameful to the Church as both a central institution in the lives of the faithful and a moral force in the secular world, and have aggravated the harm suffered by victims and their families. The bishops themselves recognized in the Charter that both the abuse itself and the response of some of the bishops to that abuse "caused enormous pain, anger, and confusion." The bishops acknowledged that "in the past, secrecy has created an atmosphere that has inhibited the healing process and, in some cases, enabled sexually abusive behavior to be repeated." Finally, the bishops stated, "As bishops, we acknowledge our mistakes and our role in that suffering, and we apologize and take responsibility for too often failing victims and our people in the past."

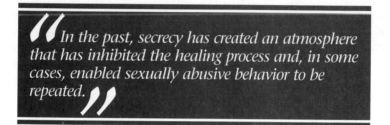

In the past, secrecy has created an atmosphere that has inhibited the healing process and, in some cases, enabled sexually abusive behavior to be repeated.

The bishops were right to recognize their part in the crisis and the extent and gravity of the crisis. The Review Board believes, however, that effective measures have been taken to ensure the safety of minors in the Church today. Actions taken by many, but not all, dioceses in the 1980s and early 1990s significantly reduced the number of reported incidents of abuse. More recently, in the wake of the Charter, several hundred abusers who had not yet been removed from ministry were laicized or otherwise removed from ministry [between March 2001 and March 2003]. Many bishops have met with victims and their families, even if belatedly, and have seen first-hand the horrific impact abuse can have on victims and their families. In addition, most dioceses have implemented safe-environment policies that train adults to recognize the signs of abuse and teach children to report it.

Moreover, the "zero-tolerance" policy embodied in the Essential Norms adopted in 2002 by the bishops in response to the crisis specifies that no priest who has sexually abused a minor will continue in ministry. To ensure that the zero-tolerance policy is applied consistently, bishops must consult with lay review boards in assessing allegations of sexual abuse of minors and making determinations about a priest's suitability for ministry.

The policies and procedures put in place [since 2002] do not remediate, nor can they excuse, the multitude of preventable acts of abuse that preceded them. But in acknowledgment of those acts of abuse as crimes and sins lies hope for the future. That hope can be fulfilled, however, only if the bishops maintain a commitment to meaningful reforms and vigilant enforcement that outlasts the immediate crisis and becomes ingrained in the character of the Church itself.

The Nature of the Crisis and Contributing Factors

Narrowly defined, the nature of the current crisis is twofold: It consists both of the sexual abuse of minors by clergy and the failure of many Church leaders to respond appropriately to that abuse. But the crisis also has a spiritual dimension, for, as is the case with all sinful conduct, it represents a failure to comport with divine law and the teachings of the Church. Unless all aspects of the crisis are addressed forthrightly, any steps to remedy it will bear only the patina of reform and renewal.

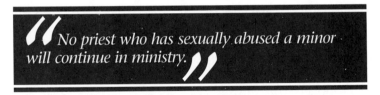

No priest who has sexually abused a minor will continue in ministry.

Although it is not possible to pinpoint any one "cause" of the problem of sexual abuse of minors by priests, there were two overarching contributing factors:

- Dioceses and orders did not screen candidates for the priesthood properly. As a result, many sexually dysfunctional and immature men were admitted into seminaries and later ordained into the priesthood.
- Seminaries did not form candidates for the priesthood adequately. As a result, seminarians were not prepared for the challenges of the priesthood, particularly the challenge of living a chaste, celibate life.

In addition, although neither the presence of homosexually-oriented priests nor the discipline of celibacy caused the crisis, an understanding of the crisis is not possible without reference to these issues. There are, no doubt, many outstanding priests of a homosexual orientation who live chaste, celibate lives, but any evaluation of the causes and context of the current crisis must be cognizant of the fact that more than eighty percent of the abuse at issue was of a homosexual nature. Likewise, celibacy does not cause sexual abuse; but the Church did an inadequate job both of screening out those individuals who were destined to fail in meeting the demands of the priesthood, and of forming others to meet those demands, including the rigors of a celibate life.

The Failure of Bishops to Respond

Perhaps even more troubling than the criminal and sinful acts of priests who engaged in abuse of minors was the failure of some bishops to respond to the abuse in an effective manner, consistent with their positions as leaders of the flock with a duty to protect the most vulnerable among us from possible predators. Sexual abuse of minors is an evil and, as one priest told the Board, knowingly allowing evil conduct to continue is "cooperation with evil." Causes of this failure include the following:

- Bishops and other Church leaders did not understand the broad nature of the problem but treated allegations as sporadic and isolated.
- Some bishops and other Church leaders often put what they erroneously believed to be the institutional concerns of the local Church above the concerns of the universal Church. The fear of scandal caused them to practice secrecy and concealment.
- The threat of litigation caused some bishops to disregard their pastoral role and adopt an adversarial stance not worthy of the Church.
- Some bishops and other Church leaders failed to comprehend fully the extent and magnitude of the harm suffered by victims of sexual abuse by priests.
- Bishops and other Church leaders relied too heavily on psychiatrists, psychologists, and lawyers in dealing with a problem that, while it undoubtedly has psychological causes and legal implications, is at its heart a problem of faith and morality.
- Bishops and other Church leaders did not do enough in the way of "fraternal correction" to ensure that their brethren dealt with the problem in an effective manner.
- Some bishops and other Church leaders placed the interests of the accused priests above those of the victims and too often declined to hear from victims directly, relying

instead on denials and assurances from those accused of abuse.

- Canon law and canonical procedures made it too difficult to remove a predator priest from ministry, and bishops did not make sufficient use of what canonical authority they did have to take action against such priests and protect the children and young people of the Church.

As a result, priests who had engaged in sexual abuse of minors were, with distressing frequency, allowed to remain where they had abused, reassigned to other parishes within the same dioceses, or allowed to live in other dioceses where they posed a further threat to children that predictably materialized into additional incidents of abuse.

Sexual abuse of minors is an evil and . . . knowingly allowing evil conduct to continue is 'cooperation with evil.'

The leniency afforded predator priests by some bishops may in some instances have been a misguided act of forgiveness. Nevertheless, the failure of some bishops to temper forgiveness with responsible actions to insulate minors from additional acts of abuse has seriously undermined the confidence of the laity in the leadership of the Church as a whole.

Recommendations for the Future

Ultimately, the crisis besetting the Church is not a legal crisis, a media crisis, or a personnel crisis, but a crisis of trust and faith; and it is only by the living out of their faith by bishops, priests, and the laity that the Church will be able to regain trust and fulfill its mission. By enacting the Charter and the Essential Norms, the bishops have laid a framework for restoring the trust of the laity in the Church hierarchy in the United States and ensuring the safety of minors in the Church. The Review Board's most urgent hope is that the bishops zealously enforce and adhere to the Charter and the Essential Norms, which then can serve as a beacon for the Church in other countries, for other churches and ecclesial communities, and for secular organizations.

But in order for the Church to achieve the goal set out by

the bishops of "restoring the bonds of trust that unite us," more must be done, through a process that involves both transparency and substantial participation by the laity. To that end, this Report offers a number of recommendations, including the following:

- *Enhanced screening, formation, and oversight.* The Church must ensure that the men selected as candidates for the priesthood in the Catholic Church are mature, well-adjusted individuals with a clear understanding of the challenges of the priesthood, including the challenge of celibacy; that candidates undergo proper formation as seminarians to meet those challenges through a process for which responsible bishops take personal ownership; and that the seminaries themselves are capable of accomplishing this mission.

- *Increased sensitivity in responding to allegations of abuse.* Church leaders must not let concerns about the rights of accused priests, the threat of scandal, and the potential adverse consequences of litigation keep them from their primary duty when faced with allegations of abuse—seeing to the welfare of victims of abuse. More openness regarding allegations and evidence of abuse, and the response thereto, is needed. Greater sensitivity to victims also requires the avoidance of harsh litigation tactics that tend to compound the pain that already has been inflicted.

- *Greater accountability of bishops and other church leaders.* The Church must choose bishops who see themselves first and foremost as pastors; and the bishops must ensure that their brother bishops act accordingly. Diocesan and presbyteral councils should be revitalized to provide an increased measure of advice and oversight for bishops; and other mechanisms, such as strengthened metropolitans, accreditation-type visitations of the dioceses, and lay diocesan consultative boards, should be considered as a means of providing greater accountability on the part of bishops and other Church leaders.

- *Improved interaction with civil authorities.* Dioceses and orders should report all allegations of sexual abuse to the civil authorities, regardless of the circumstances or the age or perceived credibility of the accuser, and should endeavor to resolve government investigations and civil claims on reasonable terms and in a manner that minimizes the potential intrusion of civil authorities into the

governance of Church matters.
- *Meaningful participation by the Christian faithful in the Church.* The bishops and other Church leaders must listen to and be responsive to the concerns of the laity. To accomplish this, the hierarchy must act with less secrecy, more transparency, and a greater openness to the gifts that all members of the Church bring to her. . . .

The John Jay College Study

The bishops, through the Charter, asked the Board to examine the causes and context of the current crisis. The Conference, through the Board, commissioned a research group at the John Jay College of Criminal Justice of the City University of New York to produce a descriptive study through a comprehensive survey of all dioceses and religious orders in the United States. These surveys requested detailed information about the number of allegations of sexual abuse of minors by priests, the nature of the alleged abuse, responses of Church leaders to allegations of abuse, and many other areas. The applicable time period is 1950 to 2002. Each diocese and religious order also was directed to report the total amount of money it had paid out to victims or alleged victims of sexual abuse during this time period, including money paid for counseling and attorneys' fees.

The survey results, some of which are summarized below, are extremely helpful in understanding the causes and context of the current crisis for the Church. By calling for and agreeing to participate in this scientific exercise, the bishops showed real leadership, and the Board urges leaders of other institutions to follow their lead so that our society can gain a better understanding of the nature and extent of child sexual abuse in the United States. . . .

Accused Priests

According to the survey data, four percent of priests who were in ministry between 1950 and 2002 have been accused of an act of sexual abuse of minors. The prevalence was highest among diocesan priests. There were 75,694 priests in diocesan ministry between 1950 and 2002. Of those priests, allegations of sexual abuse of minors had been made against 3,265, or 4.3%. By contrast, allegations of sexual abuse of minors had been made with regard to approximately 2.7% of the approximately 34,000 religious order priests in ministry during the time period. The remaining approximately 200 priests alleged to have sexually abused a minor during this period were "extern" priests; that is, priests resident in a diocese different from the diocese in which they had been incardinated.

Fifty-six percent of the accused priests had one reported allegation levied against them. Twenty-seven percent of the priests had two or three allegations levied against them. Nearly fourteen percent had four to nine allegations levied against them. Three percent had ten or more allegations levied against them; these 149 priests with ten or more reported allegations were responsible for almost 3,000 victims, or twenty-seven percent of the allegations.

Victims

Diocesan and order records identify 10,667 reports of minor victims of sexual abuse by priests. More than ten percent of these allegations were characterized as not substantiated. In addition, for approximately twenty percent of the allegations, the priest was deceased or inactive at the time of the receipt of the allegation and typically no investigation was conducted in these circumstances.

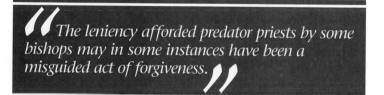

The leniency afforded predator priests by some bishops may in some instances have been a misguided act of forgiveness.

Eighty-one percent of the reported victims were male, and nineteen percent were female. The proportion of male and female victims changed over time. In the 1950s, approximately sixty-four percent of the victims were male. That percentage increased in the 1960s to approximately seventy-six percent and increased again in the 1970s to approximately eighty-six percent and remained at or near that percentage through the 1980s.

Approximately seventy-eight percent of the reported sexual abuse victims were between the ages of eleven to seventeen when the abuse began. Sixteen percent were between the ages of eight to ten, and slightly less than six percent were younger than eight years old. Thus, although more than three-quarters of the victims were between eleven and seventeen when the abuse began, a significant number of pre-pubescent children were victimized. The number of reported victims under the age of eleven has fallen each decade since the 1960s, but the fact remains that almost two thousand young children were victimized by "pedophile priests," a number that is very troubling.

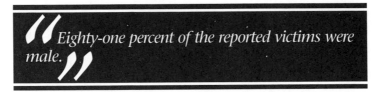

Eighty-one percent of the reported victims were male.

The majority of the victims were males between the ages of eleven and seventeen. The number of reported male victims in this age group increased from 353 in the 1950s, to 1,264 in the 1960s, to a peak of 2,129 in the 1970s. The number then decreased to 1,403 in the 1980s and 363 in the 1990s. The number of girls who have been the victims of sexual abuse by priests has varied much less over time. The total number of female victims between eleven and seventeen when the abuse began peaked in the 1960s at 305 and has decreased every decade since then.

Types of Reported Abuse

There is a tremendous range in the type of abuse reported during this time period. While all abuse is reprehensible and traumatic, the range in the type of abuse is significant. As noted above, there were 10,667 reported victimizations. Dioceses and orders were asked to indicate all of the aspects of the abuse for each victimization. Thus, a single reported victimization could involve several separate acts of abuse of varying degrees. Detailed information on the nature of the abuse was not reported for 26.6% of the reported allegations. 27.3% of the allegations involved the cleric performing oral sex on the victim. 25.1% of the allegations involved penile penetration or attempted penetration.

Responses to Allegations of Abuse

In the majority of the reported allegations when the accused priest was still living, the diocese or religious order did take

some action. Nearly forty percent of the accused priests partic-
ipated in a sexual offender treatment program. In very few
cases, however, did the diocese or order report the allegation to
civil authorities. Nevertheless, according to the data, more
than one hundred priests or former priests served time in
prison for conduct involving sexual abuse of a minor.

Although there has been a great deal of attention paid to certain cases in which a priest who had been accused of molesting
a minor took up residence in another diocese, there appear in
fact to have been relatively few such incidents. According to the
survey data, approximately 143 priests were alleged to have engaged in sexual abuse of a minor in more than one diocese.

Time Period of the Reported Abuse

The survey data are consistent with statements made by clergy,
lawyers, psychologists, and psychiatrists, indicating that the
problem of clergy sexual abuse of minors by priests significantly increased in the 1960s, peaked in the 1970s, and decreased thereafter.

According to the survey data, 9.7% of the reported allegations of abuse began in the 1950s, 26.1% in the 1960s, 35.5% in
the 1970s, 22.6% in the 1980s, and 6.2% began between 1990
and 2002. Likewise, the number of priests who were reported as
having engaged in sexual abuse of minors rose steadily in the
1960s, peaked in the 1970s, and declined sharply throughout
the 1980s and 1990s. Priests ordained in the early 1970s were
more likely to have been accused of sexual abuse of a minor
than priests ordained in any other period.

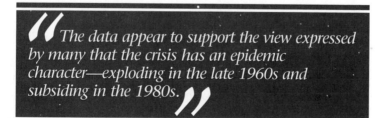

*The data appear to support the view expressed
by many that the crisis has an epidemic
character—exploding in the late 1960s and
subsiding in the 1980s.*

As noted above, abuse of males between the ages of eleven
and seventeen is primarily responsible for the spike in the incidence rate of clergy sexual abuse between the mid-1960s and
the mid-1980s. The number of male victims between the ages
of eleven and seventeen increased more than six-fold from the

1950s (with 353 victims) to the 1970s (with 2,129 victims). The number of male victims under the age of eleven increased significantly as well—more than three-fold—during the same period, from 135 to 434.

The data appear to support the view expressed by many that the crisis has an epidemic character—exploding in the late 1960s and subsiding in the 1980s. The number of reported incidents of sexual abuse of minors by priests significantly lessened after the bishops began addressing the problem more forcefully in the late 1980s and early 1990s. It must be cautioned, however, that there typically is a long lag between the occurrence of abuse and the report of that abuse, so additional allegations of abuse during that time period will be reported in the coming years. Given, however, the amount of attention paid to this issue in the last few years, and the efforts by the dioceses to identify victims, it is likely that abuse is reported more promptly today than in the past. . . .

Taking Responsibility Is the First Step Toward Renewal

In making public this report and recognizing the stain that it exposes on the Church that we love, we can but recall the Old Testament words of the psalmist who taught that while hidden guilt festers, honest admission of guilt heals:

> As long as I kept silent,
> My bones wasted away;
> I groaned all the day . . .
> Then I declared my sin to you;
> my guilt I did not hide.
> I said, "I confess my faults to the Lord,"
> and you took away the guilt of my sin.
> (Psalm 32.)

It is with that faith in the merciful powers of the Almighty that we members of the National Review Board offer the candid judgments we have been asked to give. How, one may ask, can any forgiveness, much less renewal, emerge from such a sordid history of misdeeds? We are inspired, as always, by the example of Jesus, who two thousand years ago founded this Church and who during his life on earth once instructed his disciples: "For human beings this is impossible, but for God all things are possible."

4

Law Enforcement Efforts Against Child Pornography Are Ineffective

Philip Jenkins

Philip Jenkins is a professor of history and religious studies at Pennsylvania State University and the author of Beyond Tolerance: Child Pornography on the Internet.

Law enforcement against trafficking child pornography on the Internet is weak. The current law enforcement strategy focuses on arresting individuals rather than acting against the major suppliers and trafficking institutions. In order for any real war against child pornography to be successful, journalists must be allowed to show the public some of the material child pornographers are producing. Only then will people understand the horror of child pornography and pressure politicians to improve the legal system. Such changes in policy could prevent many children from being hurt and exploited.

In the mid-1990s, a man gained access to the children in a private German or possibly Danish kindergarten. Over a period of years, he took thousands of nude photographs and videos of girls between the ages of 3 and 6. This so-called "KG" (kindergarten) series today represents one of the most prized porn collections available on the Internet. There is a still more

Philip Jenkins, "Bringing the Loathsome to Light," *Chronicle of Higher Education*, vol. 48, March 1, 2002, p. B16. Copyright © 2002 by John Philip Jenkins. Reproduced by permission.

sought-after hard-core version, "KX," in which the same children perform oral sex and masturbation upon adult men.

Trafficking in Child Porn Does Not Often Lead to Arrest

These images are freely available to anyone who wants them, provided the seeker has minimal technical expertise. And despite a common impression to the contrary, the odds that trafficking in even the hardest of kiddie porn will lead to any official sanctions are virtually nil. If the coming of the Internet has not exactly legalized child pornography of the most worrisome kind, then it has made such material extraordinarily accessible, and almost risk-free to those viewing it.

It is this amazing impunity of traffickers that first interested me in the topic of computerized child porn, which represents a critical case study for any efforts to enforce law in cyberspace. If something like KX cannot be regulated online, then what can? Although the topic cried out for examination, the legal obstacles to doing research on it initially seemed so off-putting as to forbid any kind of academic analysis. I eventually found ways to explore the subculture, however, without running afoul of the law, using methods that are anything but perfect, but which are probably the best available under the circumstances. My recently published book, *Beyond Tolerance*, records an often troubling year spent in the virtual company of some of the world's most loathsome deviants. I still really can't say whether online child porn can be eliminated. But I am sure that the methods now being deployed are failing miserably. More can be done, but only if the public recognizes just what this subculture is, and how it operates.

> More can be done, but only if the public recognizes just what this subculture is, and how it operates.

It might seem bizarre that child porn can be obtained free of penalty, in light of the frequent news reports about people being arrested for trading in such material. Yet virtually all those who fall into the hands of the authorities are the staggeringly unlucky or incompetent, those who have violated the most basic rules of electronic security and common sense. These are, for instance, the people who trade illegal images with anonymous e-friends who turn out to be police officers. In the bulletin boards and newsgroups where the serious traffickers socialize, the famous child porn "sweeps" are greeted with some humor. As one organizer of this electronic underworld—who goes by the screen name Godfather Corleone—remarks, "Looking at the enormous amount of lolita-lovers out there, very, very few get arrested, the opposite of what most newbies [novices] seem to believe is the case." Few risks face patrons who frequent child-porn newsgroups, where users collect and exchange images with impunity. I have estimated, tentatively, that the child-porn boards and newsgroups attract a regular audience that has grown to about 100,000, of whom at most a few hundred—the most inept—are likely to face legal consequences. The numbers make nonsense of the popular image of sophisticated official surveillance techniques that can home in on electronic wrongdoers on a few minutes' notice.

Child Porn Is Not Rare Online

It is ironic that I should be the one sounding alarms about child pornography, or, indeed, any moral menace. My scholarly work over the past few years has debunked exaggerated claims surrounding issues as diverse as serial murder, clergymen's abuse of children, and synthetic drugs. It was actually through such a project that I discovered the child-porn underworld.

Some years ago, I was beginning a study of Internet pornography, looking chiefly at the harmless subculture of amateur adult porn—homemade smut. At that stage, I had no intention of dealing with child porn, because I did not think that it existed in any significant quantity. When writing my previous book, *Moral Panic*, I had found overwhelming evidence that this kind of material is all but impossible to obtain through non-electronic means, and so I initially believed that it was equally rare online. But I was wrong. Child porn is a substantial presence, to the extent that a serious "fan" can easily collect 50,000 to 100,000 images, all illegal, and manufactured mainly in the past 5 to 10 years. Moreover, the material out there is more damaging than most of us would imagine, in terms of the types of activity depicted and the age of the children.

Now, after spending a decade arguing that various social

threats are vastly overblown, I find myself seeking to raise public concern about a quite authentic problem that has been neglected. This is a disconcerting position for someone who defines himself as a strong libertarian, who believes that criminal law should be kept as far removed as possible from issues of personal morality. I am anything but an antismut activist. Yet although I reject efforts to restrict sexually explicit adult material, my new book could be used as political ammunition to promote just that goal.

I realized from the start of this research that my efforts would appear paradoxical, though they really are not. The crucial difference lies in the area of consent, where a clear distinction exists between sexual material depicting adults and that focused on children. The fact that the child-pornography industry harms those who cannot give consent justifies suppressing atrocities like KX.

The Problem of Child Porn Is Difficult to Study

Once I had found the child-porn culture on the Internet, the next question was how to study it, given a legal environment in which virtually any contact with the material can lead to a federal prison sentence. "Children," for legal purposes, means anyone below the age of 18, and "pornography" includes depictions that would be only mildly indecent if adult subjects were involved. Moreover, one "possesses" an electronic image merely by downloading it, by clicking on a Web link.

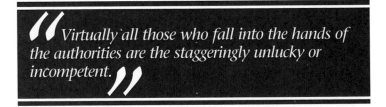

Virtually all those who fall into the hands of the authorities are the staggeringly unlucky or incompetent.

I found a solution to this methodological problem. Though all visual images in this trade are strictly prohibited, words are subject to constitutional protections. That exception allows the researcher to access the newsgroups, bulletin boards, and message boards that provide the organizing framework for the whole underground community, and which together generate thousands of words of text every day.

Often, the texts are accompanied by pictures that would be

criminal to view, but I evaded that problem simply by deactivating the "autoload images" feature of my browser software. I could thus access a page that might have contained hard-core child pornography, but all I saw on my screen were generic icons indicating that visual material was available if I decided to download it—which I did not.

> *This change would allow the news media to provide a reality check to law enforcement's claims about mounting a war against child porn.*

Now the obvious objection here is, how did I know that it was indeed child porn? Countless Web sites claim to be offering "kiddie porn" or "young Lolitas" while actually presenting nude pictures of women in their 20s or older. Fortunately for my purposes, image sites are critiqued exhaustively in the "pedo boards," which discuss at length what goes on in the pictures, the age of the subjects, and so on, and misleading claims are quickly rebutted. That kind of critical reaction leads me to believe that I can speak accurately about the nature of particular sites. Also, using the pedo boards yields an amazing amount of information about the subculture, telling us not only about the attitudes and beliefs of participants, but also how they get away with behavior that is criminalized in virtually every nation in the world.

Increased Awareness of Child Porn Is Needed

The fact that the Internet has made child pornography so widely available demands a policy response, but we have to proceed carefully. The worst outcome would be to use the nightmare of child porn to mobilize support for legislation to suppress adult or controversial material on the Internet. Such a policy would gravely threaten the usefulness of the Internet while making next to no impact on the specialized and heavily insulated child-porn subculture. We already have all the laws we need to combat child-oriented material; we just have to find a way to enforce them. Above all, that means effective cooperation between police agencies and private businesses, especially the Internet-service providers. Such cooperation has to be implemented across national boundaries.

The main lesson I drew from the study was the need to overcome our ignorance on the issue, and that is where I hope to make some contribution. Currently, the public is simply not able to evaluate police agencies' effectiveness against the manufacture and distribution of such material, because draconian laws against child porn make it all but impossible to investigate the topic.

The absence of previous studies—journalistic or academic—explains why most writers have failed even to notice the existence of this burgeoning subculture. We search the literature in vain for references even to core child-porn newsgroups. If the public does not even know that the newsgroups and bulletin boards exist, then the police face no pressure to eradicate them, with all the complex international cooperation that such an effort would demand. In many cases, moreover, police agencies simply cannot afford to hire the skilled personnel they would need to mount an effective challenge to computerized crime. Instead, police agencies can continue generating plausible statistics about the "war on child porn" by arresting the small fry they catch in obvious stings.

While child porn itself must remain criminal, we might want to think about some kind of journalistic exemption to the law, to permit access to such material in the course of a legitimate news-gathering venture (although I recognize all the difficulties of defining "legitimate"). And just why is it necessary to use the images themselves? Well, the journalist Tim Tate once said that the main reason people don't fight child pornography is that most of them have never seen it. Actual exposure to this material would galvanize public opinion—and, incidentally, would make clear the huge difference in potential harm between child porn and even the hardest of hard-core adult images.

Opening this avenue would raise the possibility of better exposing the trade, creating public awareness about its key institutions, and pressuring politicians to act against major suppliers and trafficking institutions, rather than just hapless individual consumers. If nothing else, this change would allow the news media to provide a reality check to law enforcement's claims about mounting a war against child porn. We would finally be able to see if the supply was being reduced or if—as I suspect—sporadic arrests were having no impact whatsoever. Such a policy might help forestall the arrival of the next generation of horrors like KG and KX.

5

Law Enforcement Efforts Against Child Pornography Are Effective

John Ashcroft et al.

John Ashcroft is a former U.S. attorney general. Michael Garcia is the assistant secretary of Homeland Security for Immigration and Customs Enforcement. Keith Lourdeau is the Federal Bureau of Investigation's deputy assistant director of the Cybercrime Division. Scott Christensen is a sergeant of the Nebraska State Patrol and chairman of the board of the Internet Crimes Against Children Taskforce.

The U.S. Department of Justice, the Federal Bureau of Investigation, the U.S. Immigration and Customs Enforcement Agency, and local Internet task forces are making a coordinated and aggressive effort to stop the online proliferation of child pornography. Each agency employs specially trained officers who investigate, arrest, and charge child pornographers using peer-to-peer networks to trade pornographic images of children. Arrest numbers prove the success of these task forces. The coordinated effort and systematic response of these agencies will ensure that purveyors of child pornography will not be protected by the anonymity of the Internet.

Editor's Note: The following selection is an extract from a transcript of a news conference held by the U.S. Department of Justice on the subject of child pornography.

John Ashcroft, Michael Garcia, Keith Lourdeau, and Scott Christensen, "Attorney General Ashcroft Holds Justice Department News Conference on Child Pornography," *Political/Congressional Transcript Wire*, May 14, 2004.

*J*OHN ASHCROFT: The Internet is now the marketplace for child pornography, and the Department of Justice is acting to ensure that cyberspace is not a free trafficking zone for purveyors of child pornography and predators of children.

Today [May 14, 2004,] I am announcing the results of a national law enforcement initiative that is combating the growing volume of illegal child pornography traffic through what are called peer to peer, or P2P computer networks.

Individuals in such situations are trolling the back alleys and dark corners of the Internet. They are leveraging its technology and anonymity to abuse and exploit the most innocent in our society.

Law Enforcement Response to Child Pornography Is a Coordinated Effort

This law enforcement operation launched in the fall of 2003 is an aggressive coordinated initiative combining the resources of federal, state and local law enforcement. It is part of an ongoing effort to keep pace with emerging technologies used to facilitate and to hide heinous crimes.

To date, the coordinated efforts of the Justice Department, the FBI, the United States Immigration and Customs Enforcement Agency, or ICE, and the 39 local Internet Crimes Against Children Task Forces.

These combined efforts have resulted in the execution of hundreds of searches nationwide. At last count, we have identified 3,371 suspect computers distributing child pornography through the use of peer-to-peer software over the Internet.

This law enforcement operation . . . is an aggressive coordinated initiative combining the resources of federal, state and local law enforcement.

[As of May 2004] this law enforcement operation, for which I am providing an update, has opened a total of more than a thousand domestic investigations into the distribution and possession of child pornography, executed more than 350 search warrants, and arrested and charged more than 65 individuals. This investigation remains active and ongoing.

These cases have charged not only offenses related to possession and distribution of child pornography, but also to sexual abuse of children. Further, the investigations have identified several individuals who have been convicted of sex offenses previously, as well as several registered sex offenders.

Investigators and agents from the participating agencies used several techniques, including undercover work, to infiltrate the P2P, or peer-to-peer networks, and identify those who distributed and took possession of child pornography images.

Cases That Illustrate the Law Enforcement Operation

Two cases illustrate the scope of this P2P law enforcement operation.

Investigators in California, working with the Wyoming attorney general's office, division of criminal investigation, identified an alleged peer-to-peer trafficker named "Pedokiller."

Forty-year-old Jimmy Richard Morrison of Modesto, California, allegedly had countless images of underage girls on the wall of his bedroom.

A search of his computer allegedly revealed thousands of images of child pornography, along with photos and videos from actual victims. Morrison allegedly admitted to distributing images of child pornography. Morrison was indicted in the Federal District Court of Wyoming for distribution of child pornography.

He was also charged with other criminal offenses in the Eastern District of California. The suspect is in custody in California pending trial [as of May 2004]. Earlier this week [of May 14, 2004], a federal grand jury in Houston, Texas, indicted 28-year-old Steven Allen Gardner on charges of distributing images of child pornography from his home computer and possession of child pornography.

Court documents allege that a file containing movies depicting children being sexually assaulted was available on a P2P-enabled computer at Gardner's home. Gardner is being held without bond in the Harris County, Texas jail on charges filed in Colorado of sexual assault of a 6-year-old child.

Individuals arrested and charged in this investigation are of course presumed innocent until proven guilty in a court of law.

The maximum federal sentence for the distribution of child pornography is 20 years in prison.

The PROTECT Act, signed by President Bush last spring [2003], also created a mandatory minimum sentence of five years in prison for this crime. If an individual committed a prior sex abuse offense, the mandatory minimum is 15 years in prison and the statutory maximum is 40 years.

Peer-to-Peer Networks Are Vehicles for Illegal Activity

Peer-to-peer is unlike ordinary use of the Internet where thousands of users' computers link to a main Internet server.

Peer-to-peer networks allow users, through the installation of peer-to-peer software, to go online and to connect their computers directly to one another, one computer user to another.

Peer-to-peer network members can access and download files designated for distribution directly on any of the computers that are a part of the peer-to-peer network. . . .

Peer-to-peer networks are vehicles for a great deal of illegal activity, including the theft and trafficking of music, of films, of computer games, software, as well as the illegal trafficking of child pornography.

Combating this criminal activity is a focus of the Justice Department's Intellectual Property Task Force.

The Justice Department's coordinated efforts to combat the illegal proliferation of child pornography through peer-to-peer trafficking is ongoing. There are no free rides on the information highway for traffickers of child pornography.

To those who prey on America's young and innocent, the Department of Justice will use every resource available to identify, investigate and prosecute those who traffic in child pornography, and the prosecution will be to the fullest extent of the law. . . .

I now turn to Assistant Secretary Garcia for his remarks. . . .

Immigration and Customs Enforcement's Response to Child Pornography

GARCIA: We're here today to talk about a new solution to the challenge of child pornography. In the past, the U.S. Customs Service had a long history of battling the flow of child pornography across our borders, both land borders and Internet borders.

That mission continues today, as the same dedicated and experienced investigators work these new cases in our new agency, U.S. Immigration and Customs Enforcement, or ICE, in the Department of Homeland Security.

One of the best assets we have in this fight is our cyber-crimes center, or C-3, which is located out in Virginia. This is a clearinghouse for Internet-related crimes. But we also have in C-3 a staff of specially trained forensic investigators who can follow the Internet trail, from a server in the Ukraine to somebody's hard drive in Utah.

C-3's experience includes those cases where child predators were using their credit cards to purchase child pornography online, leaving a money trail that we could follow.

And in just one case that was announced fairly recently up in New Jersey with the Department of Justice, one case involving a very finite set of providers resulted in the generation of tens of thousands of leads in this country alone, illustrating very clearly, I think, the scope of this problem.

At C-3 we are also going after users who download child pornography files directly from one person's computer—this file-swapping, peer-to-peer. We've begun an operation called Peer Pursuit in September 2003. And since that time, we've sent hundreds of leads to the field, initiated 24 investigations and made six arrests.

In one case, ICE investigators identified child pornography images being traded on a peer-to-peer network and traced the images to a man who was a volunteer for a local youth ministry program.

When our agents searched the suspect's home, they found two computers, along with audio and video equipment that had been reported stolen from the church.

And a subsequent search of that church revealed a computer there that had been used to access child pornography. The suspect later admitted to investigators that he had traded child pornography, and today [May 14, 2004] he is awaiting trial on federal charges.

But peer pursuit is just one way that ICE is targeting those who prey on children as part of our Operation Predator. Through this Operation Predator, ICE has already apprehended over 2,500 child sex predators by combining our child pornography, sex tourism and immigration authorities.

A number of these arrests were made pursuant to leads obtained through international Internet child pornography cases

ICE has made in conjunction with our law enforcement partners, many of whom are represented here today.

With the FBI and the Department of Justice and our other partners, we have created a 21st century law enforcement partnership to attack a 21st century problem. With this partnership, we are bringing the full force of U.S. law enforcement authorities and expertise to bear against those who would exploit our children.

Together, we will bring to light and bring to justice those who believe they can trade in this material in the anonymity of cyberspace. . . .

ASHCROFT: It's now my privilege to call upon the deputy assistant director of the FBI for cybercrime, Keith Lourdeau. . . .

Actions Taken by the FBI Against Child Pornography

LOURDEAU: . . . For the past few years, the FBI's Innocent Images National Initiative has led the way in combating the proliferation of child pornography and child exploitation facilitated online.

Since the inception of the program, over 3,000 subjects have been convicted. Recently, the FBI has initiated three new programs to enhance its efforts in protecting America's children: the Endangered Child Alert program, E-Groups, and Peer Pressure. The creation of these three initiatives has led the FBI to identify and rescue more than 50 victim children. During the past two years [2002–2004], we have identified a new and vastly growing problem in the dissemination of child pornography in peer-to-peer networks.

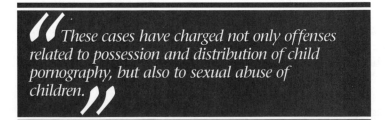

These cases have charged not only offenses related to possession and distribution of child pornography, but also to sexual abuse of children.

In response to the problem, the FBI has worked aggressively with the Department of Justice's child exploitation and obscenity section to develop protocols for investigating the transmission of these materials over these networks.

In November of 2003, the FBI initiated phase one of what we refer to as Operation Peer Pressure. During this phase, the FBI conducted 166 online sessions in which undercover agents were able to download child pornography from the offenders' computers.

It is important to note that anyone with a computer, including children, could have had the same access to these images that our undercover agents did.

The sessions resulted in the identification of 106 subjects located throughout the United States.

Using the evidence gathered during the undercover operations, agents obtained search warrants for subjects' residences where computers and other contraband were seized.

[As of May 14, 2004]: 103 searches have been executed and 17 subjects have been arrested or indicted.

Overall, 41 of the FBI's 56 field offices were involved in this first phase of Operation Peer Pressure.

It is vitally important for parents to be educated to the risks associated with peer-to-peer networking.

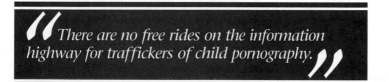

There are no free rides on the information highway for traffickers of child pornography.

While not all aspects of these networks are bad, like other Internet services, they provide pedophiles with a false sense of anonymity to collect and transmit images.

This sense of anonymity encourages pedophiles to openly share as much of their child pornography to as wide of an audience as possible.

Pedophiles will often use innocuous or popular search terms to expose innocent children and adults to graphic pornographic images. This creates a situation in which children search peer-to-peer networks for their favorite pop music artists only to find search results which include child pornography.

Parents should be aware that access to these networks is free; exposure to child pornography is not uncommon.

Let there be no doubt that peer-to-peer networks are not, and will never be, sanctuaries for those who engage in this most abhorrent crime.

We will continue to be very aggressive in pursuing those

who victimize our nation's children. The FBI continues to work closely with our local, state and federal law enforcement partners in addition to our international counterparts to address this egregious crime problem. . . .

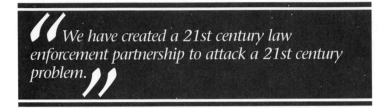

" We have created a 21st century law enforcement partnership to attack a 21st century problem. "

ASHCROFT: . . . Now I'd like to introduce Sergeant Scott Christensen of the Nebraska State Patrol; he's chairman of the board for Internet crimes against children task forces, and those task forces have active participants in this effort against child pornography. . . .

Actions Taken by Operation Peerless to Combat Child Pornography

CHRISTENSEN: . . . In March of 2003, the United States General Accounting Office issued a report on the use of peer-to-peer networks and the file-sharing technology in the distribution of child pornography.

This report was brought to the attention of the Internet Crimes Against Children Task Force (ICAC) board by Lieutenant Tom Curl of the Massachusetts State Police. At that time [March 2003], Lieutenant Curl and Special Agent Flint Waters of the Wyoming Division of Criminal Investigation, ICAC unit, saw this as an area of increased national enforcement by our 39 federally funded task forces.

Following the board meeting, Lieutenant Curl and Special Agent Waters took the initiative to develop Operation Peerless, the International Crimes Against Children initiative to combat child pornography dissemination using peer-to-peer networks.

In October of 2003, training was conducted nationally to teach task forces and ICE personnel the investigative technique designed by Special Agent Waters of Wyoming.

Special Agent Waters' technique allowed for a global uniform way of doing things for the ICAC task forces, and it assisted in investigative enforcement efforts by the task forces.

At the onset of the investigation, Special Agent Waters involved the Denver office of the U.S. Immigration and Customs Enforcement Office, and the ICE Cybercrime Center. In addition, several ICAC task forces have partnered with FBI Innocent Images task forces to combat online child exploitation.

Due to the nature of the Internet, knowing no national boundaries, this cooperative effort's instrumental in furthering these investigations in 24 foreign countries of origin that were identified.

[As of May 14, 2004], the cooperative task force investigation and Operation Peerless have resulted in the identification of over 3,000 computers used to disseminate children pornography in the P2P environment.

Of those identified, over 1,500 of these computers operate in the United States.

To date, 196 search warrants have been served, over 50 individuals have been arrested or charged, and hundreds of additional suspects have been identified.

Further investigation will result in additional warrants and the identification of users associated with the possession and distribution of child pornography. . . .

Just like instant messaging, peer-to-peer technology is used by our children and allows them to be exposed to persons and material that could harm them. The Internet Crimes Against Children task forces who carried out Operation Peerless, in coordination with our federal law enforcement partners, are to be commended for their dedication to shelter our children from this continued online exploitation.

This ongoing investigation will result in the arrest of hundreds, if not thousands, of people, who perpetrate sexual victimization of children worldwide with their thirst for images of these crimes.

The Internet Crimes Against Children task forces throughout the country will continue to strive and stay current with emerging technologies and their misuse in the exploitation of our children.

The 39 Internet Crimes Against Children regional task forces are lucky to be funded through the Office of Justice Programs, Office of Juvenile Justice and Delinquency Prevention, through the United States Department of Justice, that allows us to dedicate these efforts in the further protection of our children from online predators.

6

Child Prostitution Laws Victimize Children

Joan Ryan

Joan Ryan is a columnist for the San Francisco Chronicle.

Current laws unfairly punish child prostitutes while letting the men who exploit them escape with minimum consequences. In most cases child prostitutes are more likely to be arrested than the men who pay to abuse them. Men who solicit child prostitutes should be charged with sexual abuse, and the children they abuse should be given alternatives to street life. Advocacy groups in some cities are giving child prostitutes an alternate means of survival by providing them with food, shelter, clothing, and counseling. These much-needed services enable the girls to abandon prostitution and find a new way of life.

A 40-year-old man is caught having sex with a 15-year-old. One would expect he would be charged with statutory rape or child sexual abuse. One would expect, if convicted, he would serve hard time and have to register as a sex offender.

One would be wrong. If the 15-year-old is on a street corner in spike heels, and the 40-year-old is in a sedan with a pocketful of cash, the teenager is more likely to be locked up than the adult. She is likely to land in juvenile hall and be treated like the delinquents picked up for assault or burglary. He is likely to pay a fine, go home and spend one Saturday at an eight-hour "john school." Or the cops won't arrest him at all, telling him this is his lucky night.

Society Treats Child Prostitutes Like Criminals

We are a society that is so protective of children that we can arrest parents who don't strap their kids into car seats. We passed laws to require children to wear helmets on bikes, scooters and skateboards. We have crossing guards near their schools. We compel counselors to report any suspicion of child abuse. We levy stiff penalties on anyone who sells cigarettes or liquor to teenagers on the premise they are too young to make informed decisions on products detrimental to them.

Yet in most cities in America, a child who sells herself for sex is cast out of the protective circle of childhood. Because she is paid money, the thinking seems to go, she suddenly has the capacity to consent to her own sexual abuse. She no longer is seen as a child in need, and worthy of our protection. Adults caught paying for sex with children usually face the same charge as they do when caught with another adult: solicitation, rather than statutory rape or child sexual abuse.

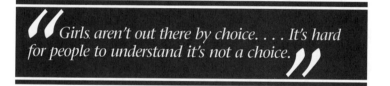

Girls aren't out there by choice. . . . It's hard for people to understand it's not a choice.

"We should be looking at it completely different," said Jasmine, who walked the streets starting at age 16, one of about 3,000 girls selling their bodies for sex in San Francisco in any one year. She asked that her real name not be used. Jasmine was put on the street by a boyfriend who brought her to San Francisco from Portland. She loved him enough to sell herself so they could pay for a hotel and food; then she hated herself enough to believe she deserved to be degraded and abused.

"Girls aren't out there by choice," she said. "It's hard for people to understand it's not a choice."

Reframing Child Prostitution as Sexual Abuse

San Francisco is taking the lead in trying to help them understand.

District Attorney Kamala Harris has promised to charge johns [men who hire prostitutes] caught with underage girls with statutory rape or sexual child abuse. "We want to erase the word 'prostitute' completely from our language when we're talking about girls," she said. "It's sexual exploitation of youth. It's child abuse for money."

Harris teamed up with Assemblyman Leland Yee, D-San Francisco, to write a bill calling for enhanced sentences for adults convicted of a sexual offense committed with a minor for money. The bill passed the Appropriations Committee on Thursday [May 27, 2004] and will be voted on by the full Assembly next week [May 30–June 5, 2004]. It then has to be passed by the Senate and signed by the governor, which could happen by midsummer [2004].[1]

The proposed law is fine as it goes. But under it, district attorneys would have to charge the adult with a sexual offense against a minor—instead of solicitation—in order to seek the enhanced sentence. And most district attorneys still treat young girls on the street as criminals instead of victims. Thus they rarely if ever file sexual abuse charges against the john.

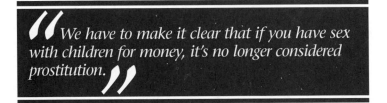

We have to make it clear that if you have sex with children for money, it's no longer considered prostitution.

San Francisco filed its first such charge just last spring [2003]. A 41-year-old man was charged with statutory rape for paying to have sex with a 14-year-old. He pleaded guilty and was sentenced to three years' probation in exchange for testifying against the girl's pimp.

"A bill like this starts to create a philosophical shift in how we respond to child prostitution," said Norma Hotaling, founder and director of SAGE [Standing Against Global Exploitation], a San Francisco advocacy group for girls and women caught in prostitution.

"We have to educate our way out of this. We have to make it clear that if you have sex with children for money, it's no longer considered prostitution. We're working with police to do good investigations so these guys don't slip through the cracks. And we have to find alternatives for kids outside the criminal justice system."

1. The bill (AB 3042) was passed by the Senate and signed by Governor Arnold Schwarzenegger in September 2004.

One alternative is a safe house where sexually exploited girls in San Francisco can find a way off the street without being locked up. It is expected to open next year [2005]. Oakland opened one last year [2003], the first city in the Bay Area to do so, following the lead of Atlanta, Los Angeles and Alberta, Canada.

Jasmine was arrested when she was 17 and spent 45 days in San Francisco's juvenile hall. Twice, she said, she avoided arrest by having sex with the cops who pulled her aside. She never witnessed a john being arrested. "The police knew I was underage, and not once did any of them offer an alternative to what I was doing," she said.

After her 45 days in lockup, where she connected with SAGE, she moved to transitional housing, where she was given food and clothing. "I didn't need to go out on the street anymore to support myself," she said.

Jasmine is 20 now, and a SAGE case manager and counselor. She spends most of her time in the familiar surroundings of San Francisco's juvenile hall. Six months ago, she met a girl who had just been picked up for prostitution. She was 11.

"These men need to go to jail because they're having sex with minors knowing that they're minors," Jasmine said. "If you give some of these guys hard sentences—real prison time, not county jail—you'd have fewer of them cruising the streets looking for young girls. Instead, the girls get locked up and continue to live a life where they're abused over and over again."

We can't have two sets of laws for children—one for the kids who have two parents and beds crowded with stuffed animals and one for the kids who have pimps and bedrolls on the floor of a hotel room. The idea of childhood sometimes seems like a chimerical thing, a pink and yellow dream we want to surround with soft pillows. There is no place in that picture for a 15-year-old girl in a black miniskirt rattling off the prices for various sex acts. She is, in that moment, the perversion of childhood.

It doesn't mean she isn't still a child.

7

Panic over Child Sexual Abuse Has Led to Unjust Civil Commitment Laws

Mark McHarry

Mark McHarry is a freelance writer. He has contributed to a number of publications, including Alternative Press Review, Bay Area Reporter, Gay Community News, *and* Journal of Homosexuality.

Civil commitment laws give states the power to commit convicted child sex offenders to mental institutions after they serve their sentences. The offenders must only be judged as having a "mental abnormality" that increases the likelihood that they will commit another sexual offense in order for the state to commit them indefinitely. Mental institutions are mandated to provide treatment but no standards for treatment exist. Therefore, in most cases "treatment" is actually nothing more than extended incarceration. Furthermore, allowing civil commitment on the basis of a simple "mental abnormality" rather than requiring a diagnosis of mental illness gives states unjustified power. The frightening reality is that civil commitment laws potentially could be used to indefinitely incarcerate any person who has been convicted of a crime.

The child-sex witch hunts of the 1980s, with their sensational allegations of human and animal sacrifice, satanic rituals, and international sex rings, have faded from public consciousness. The circus-like prosecutions such as California's

McMartin preschool and Massachusetts' Fells Acres day care center have been discredited, but they have left an odious legacy: sweeping new laws that cut deeply into what had been bedrock civil liberties.

The most draconian of these is the sexually violent predator laws. Conduct which 40 years ago might have earned a slap on the wrist now brings a life sentence in a maximum-security mental institution. But to far graver effect, the laws and the courts' opinions supporting them give states a new legal mechanism to lock up many more people than just predators.

The groundbreaking legal provision of the predator laws is the accused need not be diagnosed as mentally ill.

In effect in at least 16 states and under consideration in 21 more as of [2001], the sexually violent predator laws conflate physical violence with consensual sex with teenagers, casting a wider net than its name implies. In addition to those who commit an overtly violent act such as rape, they include merely the intention for sex between a gay-identified 17-year-old and an older partner. Despite the media characterization of predators as monsters, many of the cases prosecuted—including the landmark decision upholding the predator laws, *Kansas v. Hendricks*—involve non-violent sex with teenagers.

Predator Laws Violate Civil Rights

The predator laws are written as civil law. As such, they make an end run around safeguards against state power long part of criminal law. What's lost? The right to remain silent, to have a lawyer at interrogations, to bail, to a trial by a jury, a standard of proof of guilt beyond a reasonable doubt, the right to an appeal, among others. Fundamental constitutional protections are weakened or absent, notably double jeopardy (repeated punishment for the same crime, as well as the state's appealing an acquittal) and ex post facto (prohibiting a punitive measure created after a crime had been committed). All of these protections apply to criminal law only. Even one of the most elemental protections against arbitrary state authority, the Due Process Clause, which does apply to civil law, has been weakened.

Once committed, predators do not have the multiple layers of review other civilly committed patients do. This added review has been part of the courts' reasoning in why civil commitments—whose central purpose was not incapacitation, but self-protection and care—do not require the reasonable doubt standard of criminal law.

Despite rhetoric from state legislators and prosecutors that such laws target a very small group of highly dangerous people such as serial rapists, they are broadly written. The predator laws declare [that] those who have been convicted—in some states merely accused—of a vague array of non-violent sexual behavior represent a danger and may be held for life in a high-security mental health facility. Predator offenses include "any criminal act [found] to have been sexually motivated" (most states), "sexual misconduct" (Iowa), "individuals who, without committing an actual crime, do something sexual in nature to frighten someone else" (Missouri), and an adult touching their genitals in the presence of a child (California). Incest is often excluded. Most of the laws subject young people to predator status if they have sex with other minors. Some states can begin predator proceedings against any citizen, but most target prisoners convicted of a predator crime who have not finished their sentence or are on parole. Anyone believed to be a potential sex predator may be evaluated by a social worker or mental health employee—some states have no requirement that the evaluator be licensed—as a first step in the commitment process. All the state representative and a judge (or jury for states that use them) need do is find the accused has a personality disorder that makes them "likely," "substantially probable" or even "more likely than not" to engage in an illicit act.

For the overwhelming majority, the result is a life sentence. Though laws permit a review every one or two years, it is up to the predator to prove he or she is no longer dangerous. . . .

Mental Health Commitments

The groundbreaking legal provision of the predator laws is the accused need not be diagnosed as mentally ill. All the state need do is find that the person has an undefined mental abnormality or personality disorder which makes them likely to have illicit sex again. A "mental abnormality" or "personality disorder" is not a psychiatrically defined mental illness. It is anything a psychologist or state legislature says it is. Up to now, states have been able to commit people against their will only in the narrow situation where someone had a mental illness and was a danger to themselves or others.

Nine years ago [1992] the Supreme Court held states could not involuntarily commit to a mental institution someone considered dangerous unless they also were mentally ill. Any lower threshold for commitment—such as a personality disorder—would permit the state to lock up practically anyone. Terry Foucha had been sent to a Louisiana mental institution after being found not guilty by reason of insanity. A hospital review committee recommended he be discharged as not mentally ill, but a state court ordered him returned to the institution. The court said Foucha was dangerous on the basis of a doctor's testimony [that] he had an antisocial personality.

> *Most of those in jail have a personality disorder, and every prisoner, by virtue of having committed a crime, could be seen as dangerous.*

As Justice White wrote for the Supreme Court, most of those in jail have a personality disorder, and every prisoner, by virtue of having committed a crime, could be seen as dangerous. This rationale would permit the State to hold indefinitely any other insanity acquittee not mentally ill who could be shown to have a personality disorder that may lead to criminal conduct. The same would be true of any convicted criminal, even though he or she has completed his or her prison term. It would also be only a step away from substituting confinements for dangerousness for our present system, which, with only narrow exceptions and aside from permissible confinements for mental illness, incarcerates only those who are proved beyond reasonable doubt to have violated a criminal law. But five years after *Foucha* [1997], the Court took this step toward confinement for dangerousness in *Kansas v. Hendricks*. The Justice who wrote the dissent in *Foucha*, Clarence Thomas, authored the majority opinion in *Hendricks*. In the 5-4 decision, the Court set two new standards by which to interpret sex offender commitment statutes. In so doing, it turned the existing system of civil confinements inside out.

First, the Court held that "mental abnormality" as used in the Kansas law was sufficient to satisfy due process. Hendricks' lawyers had argued that "mental abnormality" was not equivalent to "mental illness," and thus did not meet the constitutional threshold under *Foucha*. The Court disagreed, stating "we have never required State legislatures to adopt any particular nomenclature in drafting civil commitment statutes. Rather, we have traditionally left to legislatures the task of defining terms of a medical nature that have legal significance."

Second, the Court held that the Kansas statute did not give rise to criminal proceedings, and thus confinement pursuant to the Act did not constitute punishment. This determination allowed the Court to dispose of Hendricks' *ex post facto* and double jeopardy claims. The commentary in legal and psychiatric journals afterwards ranged from unease to dismay. Many constitutional scholars are appalled the Court erased what had been a clear distinction between criminal and civil law when depriving citizens of liberty. They see states seeking, as [scholar] Eric Janus says, "the shelter of psychiatric diagnosis and civil commitment to avoid condemnation as preventive detention" when they want to lock up people whom they could not under criminal law. Psychiatrists believe the Court's opinion ruptured the status quo in which a diagnosed mental illness—as listed in the American Psychiatric Association's Diagnostic and Statistical Manual of Mental Disorders, DSM-IV—was a requirement for civil commitment.

Not Just for Predators

The chilling possibility is a similar label may await more than those who have committed violent acts or have had consensual sex with teenagers. Because the predator laws apply only to a personality disorder and because they lack the safeguards of criminal law, they give state legislatures the ability to extend indefinite confinement to any other behavior lawmakers consider deviant or delinquent.

"The term 'mental abnormality' could be used to reach all kinds of behavior that may have no relation to mental illness," says Michael Allen of the Bazelon Center for Mental Health Law. "This law would permit commitment of someone who was just maladjusted." Forensic psychologists in state mental-health departments might be happy to have expanded commitment powers, but not mainstream psychiatric organizations, which see as unethical incarceration of the non–mentally ill in a psychiatric facility.

"It's a misuse of psychiatry," says Howard V. Zonana, MD, chair of the American Psychiatric Association's task force on sexually dangerous offenders. "Once they get in, it's very hard to get out. These statutes are clearly changing the predicate of civil commitment, but only at the moment for sex offenders. But one could take hit men who have an antisocial personality disorder and say these people, too, are a public menace and how could you let them back out on the street?" "Predator" has been a term applied to hit men since at least the days of FBI director J. Edgar Hoover. But today the government is branding others as predators, including young people. A U.S. House of Representatives bill titled the "Violent Youth Predator Act" would eliminate the existing federal mandate for states to release from jails so-called status offenders. These are juveniles guilty of "crimes" such as truancy or incorrigibility, which apply only because they are not yet adults. It is not much of a leap to imagine certain types of incorrigible youth could be deemed maladjusted and potentially dangerous.

Although the Kansas statute uses both "personality disorder" and "mental abnormality" for individuals subject to confinement, it does not define personality disorder and psychologists are divided as to what merits a personality disorder diagnosis.

The result, writes Katie Isaac in the *Houston Law Review*, is future court decisions will likely determine to whom else these terms will apply. The Supreme Court is well aware of this, with some of the Justices asking during oral arguments in *Hendricks* whether a state could legitimately confine an armed robber identified as having a "sociopathic personality."

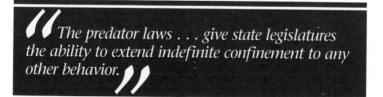

The predator laws . . . give state legislatures the ability to extend indefinite confinement to any other behavior.

Moreover, *Hendricks* allows states to link any past criminal conduct to a related "mental abnormality" or "personality disorder" in order to justify civil commitment, observes Adam Falk in *American Journal of Law & Medicine*. A state could link driving under the influence to alcohol-use disorders or, similarly, drug crimes to cocaine, hallucinogen, or cannabis-related disorders. "In this manner, a state could civilly commit all persons convicted of drug- or alcohol-related crimes. *Hendricks* provides no limitations on the scope of state power.". . .

State Mental Institutions Have No Standards for Treatment

The places where the predators are locked up are state mental hospitals, institutions that have had a dismal reputation, or in highly secure mental-health "treatment centers" under the wing of the state's prison system. Forty years ago, public pressure, including documentaries such as *Titicut Follies* and the novel *One Flew Over the Cuckoo's Nest,* exposed widespread abuses in the state mental-health institutions and helped spur a movement to release many mentally ill people to what were considered more humane community-based programs.

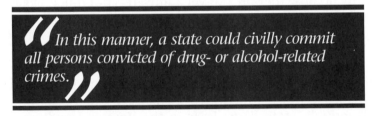

In this manner, a state could civilly commit all persons convicted of drug- or alcohol-related crimes.

But now the institutions are back, having reinvented themselves to take advantage of the need to house predators. At a time of woefully inadequate mental health care for many Americans, places like California's Atascadero State Hospital are flush with cash. Already one of the largest forensic mental institutions in the world, Atascadero is building more cellblocks and hiring staff, from psychiatric technicians to music therapists, to treat the predators. But it and the other institutions' hype about what they can do for their inmates—and treatment is a key to the courts' upholding the predator laws—has not matched their rhetoric. Worse, it appears they are repeating the same sorry story of psychiatric incompetence, patient abuse, cover-ups and resistance to outside intervention of their predecessors a generation ago. . . .

Those in charge of the institutions acknowledge the programs are experimental. Officials overseeing the Illinois mental health department say they have no idea if their treatment program is successful. This is echoed in the professional literature, with an exhaustive study by the Canadian Correctional Service reporting, "a foregone response to the question 'Does sex offender treatment work?' is this: We are still uncertain."

While those treating sex offenders admit their methods are unproven, mental health groups outside the forensic psychology community, notably the American Psychiatric Association, condemn them as ineffective and unethical.

For example, most programs use a profile called RRASOR (Rapid Risk Assessment for Sexual Offense Recidivism) to gauge whether a person should be labeled a predator, and if they are, whether they will recidivate if set free. RRASOR and its successor Static 99 were designed by a prison official, Karl Hanson. They employ a meta-analytic technique to look at published reports on sex offender recidivism, creating a sheen of statistical objectivity to complement what are generally seen as subjective and inaccurate clinical judgments.

Such profiles are a long way from accepted science. They are based on only a few recidivism reports. Their risk-predictor variables, a majority of which target male homosexuals, are derived from police reports that are inaccurate, often outdated and not subject to impartial review. Hanson has not subjected RRASOR to peer-reviewed scrutiny, merely posting it to a Canadian government website. Leading psychiatrists condemn the profiles. Dr. Fred Berlin, founder of the Johns Hopkins Sexual Disorder Clinic and associate professor of psychiatry at Johns Hopkins Hospital, has said he is "very concerned" about using such tests to deny someone their freedom: "You can use it and be 100 percent wrong . . . if psychiatrists are making determinations in that manner, they are acting improperly. . . ." At least one court has banned Static 99 due to Berlin's testimony, the judges ridiculing the test.

> *Hype about what they can do for their inmates . . . has not matched their rhetoric.*

RRASOR may be new but many of the institutions' practices have not changed much since the 1960s. Among the protocols at Atascadero and other facilities: Crude behavior-modification techniques designed to recondition inmates by describing erotic scenes while flooding them with ammonia fumes.

Unapproved drugs such as Lupron lower the predators' desire for sex. Lupron is a new class of pharmaceutical whose sole approved use is for endometriosis. Its debilitating side effects have generated controversy in the short time it has been on the market, including the establishment of a National Lupron Victims Network. It is the drug of choice to use on predators because of a handful of reports in the medical literature claiming it suppresses sex fantasies better than the safer and more proven anti-androgens used by cancer patients and gender-variant individuals. Use of a controversial device, the penile plethysmograph, to assess deviant arousal. Even the corrections community notes its inaccuracy and unreliability, the lack of an accepted methodology with which to gauge results in an individual over time, and complaints it is readily circumvented.

Thought Control

Another practice that has not changed but that has gotten more thorough is thought control. Some institutions now instruct their psychiatric aides and other custodians to monitor predators around the clock—including their off-the-cuff remarks and choice of spare-time reading material—for any evidence they might not fully believe what the treatment program is preaching.

By necessity the systems for implementing predator laws are designed to detect and punish beliefs. In the absence of objective methods, belief is the only way the state has to determine whether a predator has changed and may be released.

Criminal prison inmates may believe what they wish and to a certain extent act on it, e.g., protest their innocence and file court petitions in their defense. For someone declared a predator, any attempt to assert their beliefs locks them in an ideological battle with the state. No matter for those committed as child molesters that there is a body of evidence—small and hotly contested—which asserts sex between minors and adults is not necessarily harmful. Any attempt for a predator to rationalize his or her conduct is to deny it, and denial is considered non-compliance with treatment.

Instead, predators must prove a negative, namely that there be no doubt they are no longer dangerous. This is a tough standard to meet. To prove a negative one must do so absolutely. Any doubt means they might commit another crime. . . .

The number of people committed as predators, now [in

2001] in the several hundreds, is likely to rise to tens of thousands within a few years given the steady inflow and "no exit" policies of the states' programs. Buttressed by laws requiring licensed professionals and those holding specified jobs to report illicit sex, backed by expanded social work/mental health/police resources and taking advantage of missing criminal-law protections, there is no doubt more people will be incarcerated indefinitely.

But of greater concern is the line we cross when we lose fundamental constitutional protections. All of the rights eroded by *Hendricks* are important, but perhaps none as much as due process. Part of the "great safeguards which the law adopts in the punishment of crime and the upholding of justice," it stretches back centuries, from the Egyptians to the Aztecs, seen in every civilization that pretends to rule of law. It means fundamental fairness, preventing the State from using its awesome power arbitrarily. It is an essential moral underpinning to our democracy, part of the compact that obligates the State to safeguard the right to live freely.

The Supreme Court's *Hendricks* decision allows states to find an individual can control his or her conduct for the purpose of criminal confinement, yet can not control the exact same conduct for the purpose of civil commitment. This switches off what were bright standards limiting when and how the government can confine people. It gives the State a broad new opening under law to confine its citizens. It remains to be seen if the line has been drawn at predators or if the government will move to lock up others thought to be maladjusted and dangerous. It is disturbing to know it has the power to do so.

8

Satellite Tracking of Sex Offenders May Be More Effective than Civil Commitment

Lori Montgomery and Daniel LeDuc

Lori Montgomery and Daniel LeDuc are staff writers for the Washington Post.

The news that nine-year-old Christopher Lee Ausherman had allegedly been murdered by newly released sex offender Elmer Spencer Jr. renewed the debate over the civil commitment of sex offenders in the state of Maryland. Advocates of civil commitment assert that confining and treating violent sex offenders after they serve their sentences is the only way to prevent tragedies such as Christopher's death. Critics of civil commitment argue that the laws violate the civil liberties of those who have already been punished. They also criticize the enormous cost of housing and treating predators. Satellite tracking of released sex offenders may be a viable alternative to civil commitment. Satellite tracking enables authorities to pinpoint the movement and position of sex offenders twenty-four hours a day. Pilot programs using satellite tracking are in place in forty-one states, and the general consensus is that they are highly effective.

Two months after a 9-year-old Frederick boy was allegedly beaten to death by a newly released child molester [in November 2000], the Maryland General Assembly is set to consider a proposal to keep sexual predators behind bars even after their prison terms end.[1]

The legislation—sponsored by a Frederick County delegate whose district office is a half-mile from the ballfield where the boy's naked body was discovered Nov. 20—would compel authorities to identify the most violent sex offenders before they are released from prison. Instead of being freed, those felons would be confined for treatment until they were no longer a danger to society, or for the rest of their lives.

The proposal faces tough opposition from civil libertarians and some state officials troubled by the seeming unfairness—and enormous cost—of incarcerating people who have served their sentences.

> *In our current system, people like Elmer Spencer are going to get out. It's our obligation to make sure those people don't get out.*

Public safety and mental health officials have created a task force to study alternatives to civil commitment, including high-tech programs that force sex offenders to submit to regular lie detector tests or to 24-hour satellite tracking as a condition of probation or parole.

Elsewhere, satellite tracking has produced particularly encouraging results. In Florida, where 500 criminals carry small transmitters monitored constantly by a network of Global Positioning System satellites, parole and probation violations have dropped dramatically compared with ordinary house arrest, Florida officials said.

The system is so effective that a Daytona Beach probation agent was able to catch a child molester as he slowed his car from 46 to 28 mph last summer [2000] to watch a 5-year-old girl he had previously abused frolic in an above-ground pool.

In a recent interview, Maryland Lt. Gov. Kathleen Kennedy Townsend expressed a preference for satellite tracking, calling it "an idea worth exploring." Next month [February 2001], the

1. As of July 2004, the state of Maryland has not passed civil commitment legislation.

University of Maryland will launch a pilot program using satellites to track a small number of juvenile offenders upon their release from institutions.

Authorities also are eager to examine polygraph testing for sex offenders. Now used in 33 states, lie detector tests have been shown to help agents probe the minds of sexual predators, eliciting honest answers to questions about improper thoughts and surreptitious visits to playgrounds or pornographic Web sites.

"The experience with civil commitment in other states has involved huge expense and endless litigation focusing on a relatively small number of offenders, with treatment costs exceeding $100,000 per offender," said Leonard A. Sipes, spokesman for the Maryland Department of Public Safety and Correctional Services, which formed the task force in partnership with the state Department of Health and Mental Hygiene.

"The question for us is, do we focus on a handful of people under civil commitment or on a broader community effort?" Sipes said. "Do we focus our resources on 20, 30 or 40 offenders, or on hundreds?"

That question gained new urgency after the killing and sexual assault of Christopher Lee Ausherman, whose body was discovered six days after Elmer Spencer Jr., 45, was released from prison. Spencer, who served 3½ years of a 10-year sentence for what was at least his third attack on a child, could face the death penalty if convicted of Christopher's killing.[2]

The case horrified [state delegate] Sue Hecht (D-Frederick), who has been pushing Maryland to adopt a civil commitment law for sex offenders since 1998.

Hecht, the former director of a domestic violence center, has brought a Kansas couple to testify on behalf of her measure— the parents of Stephanie Schmidt, 19, whose killing prompted Kansas to enact its civil commitment law in 1994. This year [2001], Hecht plans to invite Christopher's mother to testify.

"Now, unfortunately, we have a face, a name, a story" in Maryland, said Hecht, who is still drafting this year's legislation.

"In our current system, people like Elmer Spencer are going to get out. It's our obligation to make sure those people don't get out," Hecht said.

Since 1990, 16 states, including Virginia, have adopted civil

2. Elmer Spencer Jr. was convicted of the murder of Christopher Ausherman in February 2002. Spencer was later sentenced to life in prison without parole.

commitment laws for sex offenders—usually because of some gruesome crime, said Scott Matson, research associate at the Center for Sex Offender Management in Rockville. The Virginia law, passed in 1999, has not been implemented because lawmakers failed to budget money for treatment programs.[3]

The laws are abhorred by civil libertarians, who say they impose further punishment on people who have paid their debt to society.

"If somebody serves their time, isn't that supposed to be enough?" said Del. Sharon Grosfeld (D-Montgomery), chairman of the House subcommittee on criminal law, which will consider Hecht's bill.

The U.S. Supreme Court, however, has upheld the laws, ruling in a challenge to the Kansas measure in 1997 that civil commitment does not violate the Constitution's prohibition against double jeopardy so long as the purpose is to treat rather than to punish.

Last week [January 17, 2001], the court voted 8 to 1 to affirm Washington state's civil commitment law, the first in the nation. The law had been challenged by a six-time rapist who claimed he was not receiving meaningful treatment.

Nationwide, [as of January 2001] 894 sexual predators have been involuntarily committed to psychiatric hospitals. Authorities have judged just 44 to be "cured" and permitted their release.

Therein, some argue, lies the problem with civil commitment.

"You can't cure a sex offender," said Richard B. Rosenblatt, director of mental health programs in the Maryland prison system. "You manage a sex offender. You help the sex offender manage himself."

To that end, satellite tracking is winning fervent applause in pilot programs in 41 states. Colorado expects to have 500 people on satellite tracking by [the end of 2001]. And Texas has enacted a civil commitment law that allows judges to substitute satellite tracking for confinement in a mental institution.

Florida has the largest program, using satellite tracking primarily for sex offenders placed on probation. Since 1998, about 8 percent of criminals monitored by satellite have violated the conditions of probation, compared with 13 percent on elec-

3. The state of Virginia passed a bill to fund and create a civil commitment program on April 4, 2003. The bill provides $2.7 million to confine and treat sexually violent predators when their criminal incarceration comes to an end.

tronic monitoring and 25 percent under ordinary house arrest, according to the Florida Department of Corrections.

The system works by requiring a criminal to wear an anklet that cannot be removed. The satellite transmitter—about the size of two videotapes—must remain within a few feet of the anklet at all times, usually in a backpack or fanny pack.

Thus outfitted, a criminal is tracked by satellite 24 hours a day and his movements stored in a computer. The transmitter alerts authorities if the criminal is not where he is supposed to be—for example, at work by 8 A.M. And it will tell them if he is somewhere he shouldn't be—loitering near a playground, for example. Settings within the transmitter immediately alert the criminal and the satellite monitoring company when he has crossed the barrier. That alert is relayed to authorities and, potentially, the victim.

The technology, which costs $9 per day per criminal, also allows agents to create "hot zones" around the homes and workplaces of victims or any other geographic location likely to be a target, such as a schoolyard or ballfield. Victims can also be given pagers that sound an alarm if the criminal comes within a certain distance of their homes.

"I like it because we have the ability to protect victims," said Kelley Shotwell, a Volusia County, Fla., probation agent who helped send a 60-year-old pedophile back to jail after his tracking device caught him driving slowly past the home of his 5-year-old step-granddaughter in July. "We knew immediately when he went into the hot zone," Shotwell said.

Despite the apparent success of such programs, some in Maryland believe only incarceration can adequately protect the public. On Thursday [January 18, 2001], [Maryland] Attorney General J. Joseph Curran Jr. (D) traveled to Larned, Kan., to visit that state's facility for sexual predators.

"The bottom line is I walked away believing there are people who do these sexually deviant acts . . . and, even at the end of their incarceration, that deviant behavior doesn't go away in some cases," said Curran, who supports Hecht's legislation.

"I realize there are civil liberties concerns. At the same time," Curran said, "I'm persuaded that there is a need to do this."

Sex Offender Registration Laws Protect Children

David Tell

David Tell is the opinion editor for the Weekly Standard, *a national newsmagazine.*

Sex offender advocates and civil liberties groups continually challenge the constitutionality of sex offender registration laws. Upon release, sex offenders are required to register with local law enforcement. Names, addresses, photographs, and descriptions of their crimes are then made available to the public. Released offenders argue that they are being denied their rights to privacy. They also assert that online registration continues to punish them after they have served their sentences. These arguments should not dissuade the courts from providing society with needed protections. It is not possible to accurately determine on a case-by-case basis which perpetrators are most likely to reoffend. Therefore, laws requiring that all sex offenders register must be upheld in order to prevent the heinous crimes that predators commit against children.

Early one evening in September 1986, a 17-year-old local girl was walking along West North Street in Wooster, Ohio, a rural town about 50 miles southwest of Cleveland, when Joel Douglas Walton Yockey, 30, also of Wooster, rolled up next to her in a pickup truck and asked if she'd like a ride. Thinking she recognized Yockey as the man who did janitorial work at her church, the teenager accepted the offer. But Yockey was not her church janitor, as it happened, and he did not take her where she wanted to go. Instead, he drove her to a cornfield near his parents' house west of town, told the girl he'd kill her if she made any noise, and then sodomized and raped her. After it was over, Yockey took his victim back to West North Street, handed her a $10 bill, and pushed her out of the truck with a warning that next time she should take a cab. For this crime—and for his remorselessness about it; Yockey insisted that the girl had "come on" to him—he was given a maximum prison sentence of 10 to 25 years.

The Model Prisoner

By all accounts and to all appearances, however, Yockey spent the next 15 of those years doing everything possible to turn his life around. He recanted his trial testimony and acknowledged responsibility and regret for the rape. He joined a series of ad hoc self-improvement workshops: "Convicts Against Sexual Abuse," for example, and the "Power Rapists Group." He completed a more formal, 18-month sex abusers treatment program in 1990, and went on thereafter to earn an associate of arts degree from Ashland University even while holding down a full-time job as groundskeeper in the Chillicothe Correctional Facility's horticultural department. Joel Douglas Walton Yockey, in other words, became a model prisoner. And on that basis—given that he had "family support and a reasonable plan including employment possibilities"—the Ohio Parole Board voted this past January [2002] to approve Yockey's release.

By March he was back in Wooster, living with his parents on Porter Drive. One street over, on North Smyser Road, their backyard almost touching the Yockeys' place, Mark and Sharon Jackson were raising two teenage daughters, Katie and Kristen.

Twelve weeks ago, on September 9 [2002], six months after Yockey had returned to town, the Jacksons, as a special treat, let both their girls spend the evening before a school holiday with a large group of friends at Wooster's annual Wayne County Fair, where virtually everyone in attendance was a lifelong family acquaintance and where their safety seemed thus assured. Sometime after nightfall, for no particular reason, the younger Jackson sister, Kristen, got separated from her companions in the crowd. But she was a sensible girl, and the fairgrounds were indeed under well-meaning watch by dozens of people who knew her, and many of those people vividly remember catching sight of her at around 9 P.M.: a five-foot-five-inch 14-year-old with a brown pony tail and a purple T-shirt walking toward the fair's main gate.

There, at Vanover Street, maybe a hundred yards from the spot where her recently paroled neighbor Joel Yockey had abducted another teenage girl 16 years before, Kristen Jackson was shortly due to meet her mother. Mere minutes later, Sharon Jackson arrived on schedule for this rendezvous. But by then her daughter had gone missing.

No doubt you have already guessed how this story will end. And your guess is correct, which fact might mercifully obviate the need to recount the rest of the thing in such grisly, slow-motion detail—but for a coincidence of the U.S. Supreme Court docket that suddenly accords this kind of grisly detail a more than ordinary public policy relevance. Specifically: The High Court has just heard [in 2002], and some time in the next few months will decide, two cases out of Alaska and Connecticut that threaten to invalidate a nationwide system of law designed to protect tens of millions of Americans, women and children primarily, just like Kristen Jackson, from hundreds of thousands of other Americans, recently paroled sex offenders, who either are—or are not—just like Joel Douglas Walton Yockey.[1] The central question is whether it is possible to make reliable, individualized predictions about how such men will behave once they've been released from prison. And, if it is, whether it is constitutional for us to keep tabs on the "safe" ones, too, just in case.

The Constitutionality of Megan's Law

At issue are the "Megan's Law" statutes all 50 states have enacted since 7-year-old Megan Kanka of Hamilton Township, New Jersey, was raped and murdered by a paroled pedophile in 1994. Their application and requirements vary from one juris-

1. On March 5, 2003, in *Connecticut Department of Public Safety v. Doe*, the U.S. Supreme Court upheld Connecticut's sex offender registration law that requires information on all sex offenders—currently dangerous or not—to be publicly disclosed. Therefore, the state of Connecticut is not required to evaluate sex offenders on a case-by-case basis to determine a danger level before requiring them to register. Rather, all sex offenders, by virtue of having been convicted of a sex crime, must register.

diction to the next, but generally speaking these laws oblige released sex offenders to register their whereabouts with local law enforcement agencies, which are obliged, in turn, to provide some degree of community notification about the neighborhood presence of said registrants. There is quite a bit of powerfully affecting anecdotal evidence that the Megan's Law mechanism has already prevented some truly ghastly crimes: mothers who glance at a Post Office billboard flyer about a convicted child molester only to see the face of their elementary school's bus driver—that sort of thing. Nevertheless, administering the system has proved vastly more difficult than anyone anticipated.

For one thing, cash-strapped city and county police agencies, especially in the larger states, are fighting a desperate and only half-successful battle to stay current with their ex-offender caseloads, a task ironically—and significantly—complicated by the law itself: Many parolees subject to sex-offender registry supervision keep more or less permanently on the move precisely to avoid the intense public scorn and embarrassment that registration necessarily entails.

And then, even more important, there are the lawsuits, which have kept countless Megan's Law programs bottled up in court, and enjoined from functioning in the first place, for years on end. Almost always, sex offender plaintiffs raise two basic constitutional complaints, both of which are squarely presented in the Alaska and Connecticut cases now [in December 2002] before the Supreme Court.

> *There is quite a bit of powerfully affecting anecdotal evidence that the Megan's Law mechanism has already prevented some truly ghastly crimes.*

To some extent at least, nearly every state now applies its Megan's Law retroactively. In other words: Certain people convicted of certain crimes committed even before the registry statute was enacted are nevertheless required to comply with its terms. Which not infrequently means that they must assist in their own public identification as sex offenders, sometimes for the rest of their lives. Two Alaskan gentlemen named "John

Doe," each of them a former prison inmate sentenced in the early 1980s for first degree sexual abuse of his minor daughter, argue that their state's Megan's Law, adopted only in 1994, represents an after-the-fact additional punishment for crimes whose then-legally-authorized consequences they have already paid. Article I, Section 10 of the federal Constitution, they point out, bars any state from passing such an "ex post facto" statute; Megan's Laws like the one in Alaska must therefore fall.

High rates of sex-crime recidivism are no fantasy.

This is not quite so neat a constitutional talking point as memories of fifth-grade civics class might lead you to believe. The ex post facto clause implicates only legislative enactments of a punitive, criminal character. States may pass retroactively applicable laws for non-punitive, civil purposes like public safety, even when the operation of those laws is triggered exclusively by past criminal activity, without offending the ex post facto clause one bit. In April of last year [2001], the Alaska John Does managed to persuade the 9th U.S. Circuit Court of Appeals that Juneau's version of Megan's Law, though explicitly designed simply to provide the public with future protection against sexual predators, is effectively, and thus unconstitutionally, a vindictive, look-back punishment for ancient misdeeds. This, first, because the statute imposes "drastic" and "onerous" liberty restrictions on the Does—purportedly requiring them to make in-person police station appearances to verify their residential and business addresses, four times a year until they die. And, second, because the law's reach is "exceedingly broad," sweeping these two men into its crude "sex offender" designation, on the basis of a little father-daughter incest business many moons ago, without ever giving the designees an opportunity to demonstrate that they no longer pose a threat to anybody.

On appeal to the Supreme Court, Alaska points out that the 9th Circuit has made a rather astonishing error of statutory interpretation: No one, in fact, is ever required to make in-person address verifications under the challenged law. What's more, even if such a requirement did exist, categorical civil regulations of ex-felons are routine and ubiquitous in our federal and state code books, and the Supreme Court has never used the ex post facto clause to strike down a single one of them. Which is why, all across the country, paroled murderers are ineligible for gun permits as a class—and nobody thinks that some panel of psychiatrists should have a case-by-case say about whether the rule is fair.

For good or ill, however, there are people who think that psychiatrists and suchlike experts should have a say in the legal status of paroled rapists and pedophiles. And it is this view, packaged more precisely and interestingly as a Fourteenth Amendment due process claim, that the Supreme Court confronts in the Connecticut Megan's Law case. Here we meet yet another "John Doe" plaintiff. Once upon a time he was sentenced to prison for an unspecified "sexually violent offense." But though he has since been released and claims to be rehabilitated, the state of Connecticut persists in calling him a "sex offender" and compounds the insult by broadcasting its judgment—39 other states and the District of Columbia do this, too—on the Internet. Sure, Mr. Doe concedes, as he must, that technically speaking he is a sex offender. But when the government reports this information to the entire world, Doe complains, it is also defaming him: implicitly labeling him an ongoing public menace while denying him any chance to disprove the charge.

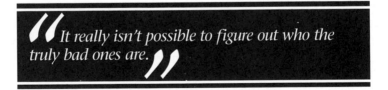

It really isn't possible to figure out who the truly bad ones are.

Last year [2001] the 2nd U.S. Circuit Court of Appeals agreed with Doe and partially enjoined Connecticut's Megan's Law. Here again, though, the constitutional question is a tricky one. As a strict procedural matter, this John Doe was surely provided all the Fourteenth Amendment process he was ever due way back when a criminal-court jury of his Connecticut peers, no doubt observing every legal nicety, judged him guilty and sent him up river for a "sexually violent offense." And as a matter of so-called "substantive" due process, the present-day residue of Doe's old conviction—Connecticut's public announcement that he is a "sex offender"—cannot, on its face, be defamatory because it is plainly true.

However, insofar as the unvarnished truth about John

Doe's past, officially sanctioned and attached to a public safety alert, indelibly signals that he is still a danger to his fellow man, then that warning might well be unconstitutionally defamatory, we suppose. Provided, that is, as Fourteenth Amendment due process doctrine requires, that the warning is "capable of rebuttal." Or, in the vernacular: If it is possible for the John Does of America to prove that they aren't any longer dangerous, then Megan's Law programs that automatically brand them with that scarlet letter are not just imperfectly successful because difficult to administer—they are an injustice.

Determining Which Offenders Pose a Threat Is Not Possible

This is the bottom-line question, then: Is it indeed possible to determine, one by one and dependably, which exconvict rapists and pedophiles remain a threat worth calling to the attention of their neighbors, and which ones do not? The various Messrs. Doe and their allies insist that it is. The Alaska Does contend that an "untrained, uninformed public" has been sold a scientifically "unsupported" fantasy about "high rates of recidivism" among sex offenders. Connecticut's Doe complains that his state's Megan's Law "ignores the ability of offenders to be successfully treated." On this Doe's behalf, the New Jersey state public defender brags that he and other "attorneys throughout the United States have become expert in rationally classifying offenders according to their relative likelihood of reoffense." And the Massachusetts Committee for Public Counsel Services, tossing a great mass of numbers around like confetti, demands that "incontrovertibly rehabilitated former offenders" be given back their reputations whole, unblackened by the "harsh" ostracism of Megan's Law obloquy.

Trouble is, all of this is demonstrably false. High rates of sex-crime recidivism are no fantasy, alas. The crimes themselves are "grossly underreported," according to the American Psychiatric Association, and consequently most conventional measures of recidivism and treatment outcome "are flawed." Even so, the best modern research on the subject is genuinely terrifying. A 1997 longitudinal study, using sophisticated statistical "survival analysis," reported that 52 percent of child molesters and rapists released from state custody in Massachusetts over a 25-year period were rearrested for a sex crime—on average, in less than four years. And every one of these people had previously been found "no longer sexually dangerous" by the Massachusetts state agency charged with adjudicating such things. It really isn't possible to figure out who the truly bad ones are.

It wasn't possible with Joel Douglas Walton Yockey, after all.

Ohio has the kind of Megan's Law that the John Does claim to approve. Ohio inspects and rates—on a three-tiered scale of dangerousness—each and every one of its incarcerated sex offenders before it grants them parole. Ohio's parole board interviewed Yockey not once but three separate times, and subjected him to an independent psychiatric examination. Then and only then did Ohio feel secure enough to conclude that Yockey's "risk to reoffend" was sufficiently minimal that he could safely be shipped home to Wooster this past March [2002]. And that no one else in Wooster, save the sheriff, need be told about it.

On September 13 [2002] FBI agents running down hunches on a case that had gone "very cold" searched Joel Yockey's Jeep and found its interior soaking wet from an unexplained and obviously desperate scrubdown. Hours later, after interviewing Yockey until almost midnight, Wayne County sheriff's deputies told Mark and Sharon Jackson that their daughter was almost certainly dead. On the rainy morning of September 14, Yockey's mother told a neighbor that her son had confessed, and teams of local volunteers were dispatched to five specific spots in a nearby swamp. At one of them they found Kristen Jackson's severed head. At another they found her arms and legs. Kristen Jackson's torso—law enforcement officials wept like babies when they made the announcement—was not recovered.

Case closed.

10

Pedophilia Is Linked to Homosexuality

Timothy J. Dailey

Timothy J. Dailey is a senior research fellow at the Center for Marriage and Family Studies at the Family Research Council. He is also the author of Dark Obsession: The Tragedy and Threat of the Homosexual Lifestyle.

Although homosexual activists have tried to distance themselves from pedophilia, evidence shows that there is a connection between the gay lifestyle and pedophilia. According to research, a much higher percentage of homosexuals sexually molest children than do heterosexuals. Defenders of homosexuality argue that men who molest boys are not attracted to adult males and therefore should not be considered homosexual. However, studies show that gay men are attracted to young adolescents and boys. Furthermore, many pedophiles consider themselves to be homosexual. Therefore, the categories of "homosexuality" and "pedophilia" that gay activists insist are mutually exclusive actually overlap.

"You shouldn't have done it. It ruined our lives!" cried a boy from the back of an Ohio courtroom as he confronted the man who sexually molested him. The perpetrator, a former Boy Scout leader, had just pleaded guilty to rape and sexual battery. As yet another example of the cycle of sexual abuse, the pedophile claimed that he too had been sexually molested as a child.

Dave, another victim of sexual molestation by a Boy Scout leader, was reduced to living on the streets when his sexual tor-

Timothy J. Dailey, "The Connection Between Homosexuality and Child Sexual Abuse," *Family Policy*, vol. 15, June 7, 2004. Copyright © 2004 by the Family Research Council, www.frc.org. All rights reserved. Reproduced by permission.

menter was finally arrested. Dave had been eating out of gar-
bage cans, running afoul of the law, and trying to numb the
terrible memories with alcohol and drugs. His life fell apart one
day as a seven-year-old boy dressed in a Cub Scout uniform,
when the Scout leader began the sexual molestation. Now sixteen, Dave is still on a path of self-destruction, and there is
seemingly little his heartbroken mother can do.

Horrific stories about the victims of child sexual abuse serve
as a lucid reminder that pedophilia is not merely an academic
issue to be debated by scholars, but a crime that destroys young
lives. In the Family Research Council's *Insight* paper, "Homosexuality and Child Sexual Abuse," we demonstrated how the
allies of the pedophile movement within the scholarly community were attempting to justify men using boys to fulfill
their unnatural sexual compulsions.

Despite efforts by homosexual activists to distance the gay
lifestyle from pedophilia, there remains a disturbing connection between the two. While many homosexuals may not seek
young sexual partners, the evidence indicates that dispropor-
tionate numbers of gay men seek adolescent males or boys as
sexual partners. The linkage of homosexuality and pedophilia
is explained in the following [article].

The Demographics of Abusers, Victims, and Homosexuals

An essay on adult sex offenders in the book *Sexual Offending
Against Children* reported: "It is widely believed that the vast
majority of sexual abuse is perpetrated by males. Indeed, with
3,000 adult male sex offenders in prison in England and Wales
at any one time, the corresponding figure for female sex offenders is 12!" This finding was echoed in a report by the American Professional Society on the Abuse of Children, which
stated: "In both clinical and non-clinical samples, the vast majority of offenders are male."

According to the *Journal of Child Psychiatry*, "contemporary
studies now indicate that the ratio of girls to boys abused has
narrowed remarkably. . . . The majority of community studies
suggest a . . . ratio . . . in the order of 2 to 4 girls to 1 boy." Indeed, the same study reports that there is likely "under-reporting
of the incidence and prevalence of sexual abuse in boys."

Relying upon three large data sets—the General Social Survey, the National Health and Social Life Survey, and the U.S.

Census—a recent study in *Demography* reported that only 4.7 percent of men and 3.6 percent of women in the United States had had even one same-sex sexual experience since age eighteen, and only 3.1 percent of men and 1.8 percent of women had had more same-sex than opposite-sex partners. Even lower figures were reported in a study of the sexual behavior of men in the United States based on the National Survey of Men (a nationally representative sample comprised of 3,321 men aged twenty to thirty-nine, published in *Family Planning Perspectives*). The study found that "2 percent of sexually active men aged twenty to thirty-nine . . . had had any same-gender sexual activity during the last ten years."

Homosexual Pedophiles Are Overrepresented in Child Sex Abuse Cases

Homosexual pedophiles sexually molest children at a far greater rate compared to the percentage of homosexuals in the general population. A study of 457 male sex offenders against children in *Journal of Sex and Marital Therapy* found that "approximately one-third of these sexual offenders directed their sexual activity against males." The author [Kurt Freund] of the same study noted in a later-article in the *Journal of Sex Research:* "Interestingly, this ratio differs substantially from the ratio of gynophiles (men who erotically prefer physically mature females) to androphiles (men who erotically prefer physically mature males), which is at least 20 to 1."

In other words, although heterosexuals outnumber homosexuals by a ratio of at least 20 to 1, homosexual pedophiles commit about one-third of the total number of child sex offenses.

Similarly, the *Archives of Sexual Behavior* also noted that homosexual pedophiles are significantly overrepresented in child sex offense cases: "The best epidemiological evidence indicates that only 2 to 4 percent of men attracted to adults prefer men; . . . In contrast, around 25 to 40 percent of men attracted to children prefer boys. *Thus, the rate of homosexual attraction is 6 to 20 times higher among pedophiles.*"

Are Men Who Molest Boys Really "Homosexuals"?

These three facts (that most molesters are men; relatively few men have engaged in same-sex sexual relations; yet about a third of child sex abuse cases involve men molesting boys) would seem to point inevitably to the conclusion that homosexual men, in proportion to their numbers, are far more likely than heterosexuals to be child molesters. So how do homosexual activists avoid this obvious, logical conclusion? Only by asserting that men who molest boys are not "homosexuals."

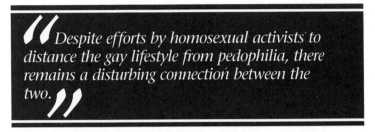

Despite efforts by homosexual activists to distance the gay lifestyle from pedophilia, there remains a disturbing connection between the two.

There is a three-fold aspect to this implausible claim. First, the defenders assert that "homosexuality" should be defined as an attraction to *adults* of the same sex, and that those who experience such attractions are *not* attracted to children.

Research, however, does not support such a sharp distinction. A study in *Archives of Sexual Behavior*, for example, found that homosexual men *are* attracted to young males. The study compared the sexual age preferences of heterosexual men, heterosexual women, homosexual men, and lesbians. The results showed that, in marked contrast to the other three categories, "all but 9 of the 48 homosexual men preferred the youngest two male age categories," which included males as young as age fifteen.

Likewise, in *The Gay Report*, by homosexual researchers Karla Jay and Allen Young, the authors report data showing that 73 percent of homosexuals surveyed had at some time had sex with boys sixteen to nineteen years of age *or younger*" [emphasis added].

The defenders of homosexuality also argue, on the other hand, that men who molest boys are generally *not* sexually attracted to adult males, and therefore should not be considered "homosexuals."

Again, however, the research does not bear out such a claim. A study of sex offenders against male children in *Behavior Research and Therapy* found that male homosexual pedophiles are sexually attracted to "males of all ages." Compared to nonoffenders, the offenders showed "greater arousal" to slides of nude males as old as twenty-four: "As a group, the child molesters responded with moderate sexual arousal . . . to the nude males of all ages." Similarly, a study of Canadians imprisoned for pedophilia in the *Journal of Interpersonal Violence* noted that some of the adult male offenders also engaged in homosexual acts with adult males.

Many pedophiles, in fact, consider themselves to be homosexual. A study of 229 convicted child molesters in *Archives of Sexual Behavior* found that "eighty-six percent of offenders against males described themselves as homosexual or bisexual."

Finally, pro-homosexual activists content that a man who molests boys but also has sexual relations with adult women— perhaps even marrying and having children—cannot be considered a homosexual. This, however, overlooks the fact that pedophiles exhibit a wide variety of sexual attractions and behavior—often to draw attention away from their primary lust for boys. A study on sex offenders in the *International Journal of Offender Therapy and Comparative Criminology* notes that "the reason child sexual abusers are successful at remaining undetected is because they do not fit a stereotype."

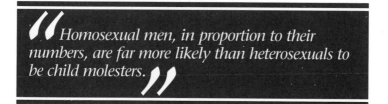

Homosexual men, in proportion to their numbers, are far more likely than heterosexuals to be child molesters.

The fact that "homosexuality" and "pedophilia" are overlapping categories, rather than mutually exclusive ones as homosexual activists argue, is demonstrated by the fact that the very term "homosexual pedophile" is common in the academic literature, having first been used in the early 20th century by the Viennese psychiatrist Dr. Richard von Krafft-Ebing, who pioneered the systematic study of sexual deviance.

Pedophilia in Gay Culture

David Thorstad, homosexual activist and historian of the gay rights movement, argues that there is a natural and undeniable connection between homosexuality and pedophilia. Thorstad writes: "Boy-lovers were involved in the gay movement from the beginning, and their presence was tolerated." The inaugural issue of the *Gay Community News* in 1979 published a

"Statement to the Gay Liberation Movement on the Issue of Man/Boy Love," which argued that "the ultimate goal of gay liberation is the achievement of sexual freedom for all—not just equal rights for 'lesbian and gay men,' but also freedom of sexual expression for young people and children."

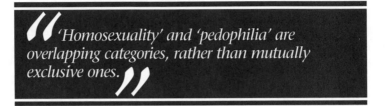

'Homosexuality' and 'pedophilia' are overlapping categories, rather than mutually exclusive ones.

Thorstad cites Jim Kepner, then curator of the International Gay and Lesbian Archives in Los Angeles:

> A point I've been trying to make is that if we reject the boylovers in our midst today we'd better stop waving the banner of the Ancient Greeks, of Michelangelo, Leonardo da Vinci, Oscar Wilde, Walt Whitman, Horatio Alger, and Shakespeare. We'd better stop claiming them as part of our heritage unless we are broadening our concept of what it means to be gay today.

In 1985 the North American Man-Boy Love Association (NAMBLA), which openly advocates "adult-child sex," was admitted as a member in New York's council of Lesbian and Gay Organizations as well as the International Gay Association—now the International Lesbian and Gay Association (ILGA). In the mid-1990's ILGA's association with NAMBLA and other pedophile groups cost the organization its status as a Non-Governmental organization in the United Nations.

Pedophile Themes Abound in Gay Literature

The late "beat" poet Allen Ginsberg illustrates the seamless connection between homosexuality and pedophilia. Biographer Raymond-Jean Frontain has written about Ginsberg's "involvement with the controversial North American Man/Boy Love Association" and "the pattern of references to anal intercourse and to pederasty that emerged" from a reading of his works.

Ginsberg was one of the first of a growing number of homosexual writers who cater to the fascination with pedophilia in the gay community. Mary Eberstadt, writing in the *Weekly Standard*, has documented how the taboo against sex with children continues to erode. Revealingly, the examples she provides of pedophilia in current literature come from gay fiction.

Eberstadt cites the *Village Voice*, which states that "Gay fiction is rich with idyllic accounts of 'intergenerational relationships,' as such affairs are respectfully called these days." She lists numerous examples of pedophilia-themed gay fiction that appear in "mainstream" homosexual anthologies. *The Gay Canon: Great Books Every Gay Man Should Read* features novels containing scenes of man-boy sex. One such book features a protagonist who is "a pedophile's dream: the mind of a man in the body of a boy." Yet another anthology of homosexual fiction, *A History of Gay Literature: The Male Tradition*, published by Yale University Press, includes "a longish chapter on 'Boys and Boyhood' which is a seemingly definitive account of pro-pedophile literary works."

Adult-youth sex is viewed as an important aspect of gay culture.

A significant percentage of books that have appeared on the Gay Men's Press fiction bestseller list contain pedophilia themes. Titles include *Some Boys*, described as a "memoir of a lover of boys" that "evokes the author's young friends across four decades"; *For a Lost Soldier:* the story of a sexual relationship between a soldier and an eleven-year-old boy; and *A Good Start, Considering:* yet another story about an eleven-year-old boy (1) who suffers sexual abuse but is rescued by a teenager who "offers him love and affection." One book published by the nation's largest gay publisher, Alyson Publications, is called *The Age Taboo*, and claims: "Boy-lovers . . . are not child molesters. The child abusers are . . . parents who force their staid morality onto the young people in their custody."

Some homosexual commentators have candidly admitted that an inordinate fascination with pedophilia exists within the gay community. Lesbian columnist Paula Martinac, writing in the homosexual newspaper *Washington Blade*, states:

> Some gay men still maintain that an adult who
> has same-sex relations with someone under the le-

gal age of consent is on some level doing the kid a
favor. . . . Adult-youth sex is viewed as an important aspect of gay culture. . . . This romanticized
version of adult-youth sexual relations has been a
staple of gay literature.

Martinac adds that:

When some gay man venerate adult-youth sex as
affirming while simultaneously declaring 'We're
not pedophiles,' they send an inconsistent message to society. . . . The lesbian and gay community will never be successful in fighting the pedophile stereotype until we all stop condoning sex
with young people.

The Consequences of Homosexual Child Abuse

Perhaps the most tragic aspect of the homosexual-pedophile
connection is the fact that men who sexually molest boys all
too often lead their victims into homosexuality and pedophilia. The evidence indicates that a high percentage of homosexuals and pedophiles were themselves sexually abused as
children. The *Archives of Sexual Behavior* reports:

One of the most salient findings of this study is
that 46 percent of homosexual men and 22 percent
of homosexual women reported having been molested by a person of the same gender. This con-
trasts to only 7 percent of heterosexual men and 1
percent of heterosexual women reporting having
been molested by a person of the same gender.

Another study of 279 homosexual/bisexual men with AIDS
in the *Journal of the American Medical Association* reported:
"More than half of both case and control patients reported a
sexual act with a male by age 16 years, approximately 20 percent by age 10 years."

Noted child sex abuse expert David Finkelhor found that:

Boys victimized by older men were over four times
more likely to be currently engaged in homosexual activity than were non-victims. The finding
applied to nearly half the boys who had had such
an experience. . . . Further, the adolescents them-

selves often linked their homosexuality to their sexual victimization experiences.

The circle of abuse is the tragic legacy of the attempts by homosexuals to legitimize having sex with boys. For too many boys it is already too late to protect them from those who took advantage of their need for love and attention. All too many later perpetuate the abuse by themselves engaging in the sexual abuse of boys. Only by exposing the lies, insincere denials, and deceptions—including those wrapped in scholastic garb— of those who prey sexually on children, can we hope to build a wall of protection around the helpless children among us.

11

Pedophilia Is Not Linked to Homosexuality

Gregory M. Herek

Gregory M. Herek is a professor of psychology at the University of California at Davis and a recognized authority on the problem of prejudice against gays and lesbians. He is also a consulting editor for three professional journals: Personality and Social Psychology Bulletin, *the* Journal of Sex Research, *and the* Journal of the Gay and Lesbian Medical Association.

Antigay activists have often accused gay people of being likely child molesters. Although the percentage of Americans who believe this myth about gay people appears to be decreasing, there is still a lot of misunderstanding. Part of this confusion is due to the use of misleading terms such as "homosexual molestation." This term is intended to describe the sexual abuse of boys by men. Unfortunately, it also conveys the assumption that the offender has developed an adult sexual orientation. In reality, most child molesters have not developed an adult sexual orientation and do not have the ability to engage in a mature sexual relationship. For these "fixated offenders," sexual attraction is based on age rather than gender. Research has failed to prove the hypothesis that homosexual men are more likely than heterosexual men to molest. Moreover, there is no data to support the assumption that gay men should not be trusted in positions of authority over children. Most researchers of child sexual abuse agree that no link between homosexuality and pedophilia exists.

M embers of disliked minority groups are often stereotyped as representing a danger to the majority society's most vulnerable members. Historically, Black men in the United States were often falsely accused of raping White women, and commonly lynched as a result. Jews in the Middle Ages were accused of murdering Christian babies in ritual sacrifices.

In a similar fashion, gay people have often been portrayed as a threat to children. When Anita Bryant campaigned successfully in 1977 to repeal a Dade County (FL) ordinance prohibiting antigay discrimination, she named her organization "Save Our Children," and warned that "a particularly deviant-minded [gay] teacher could sexually molest children."

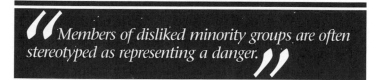

Members of disliked minority groups are often stereotyped as representing a danger.

In recent years, antigay activists have routinely asserted that gay people are child molesters. This argument has often been raised in debates about the Boy Scouts of America's policy to exclude gay scouts and scoutmasters. It has also been raised in connection with recent scandals about the Catholic church's attempts to cover up the abuse of young males by priests. Indeed, the Vatican's early response to the 2002 revelations of widespread Church cover-ups of sexual abuse by priests was to declare that gay men should not be ordained.

Public Belief in the Stereotype

The number of Americans who believe the myth that gay people are child molesters appears to be decreasing. In a 1970 national survey, more than 70% of respondents agreed (either *strongly* or *somewhat*) with the assertions that "Homosexuals are dangerous as teachers or youth leaders because they try to get sexually involved with children" or that "Homosexuals try to play sexually with children if they cannot get an adult partner."

By contrast, in a 1999 national poll, the belief that most gay men are likely to molest or abuse children was endorsed by only

19% of heterosexual men and 10% of heterosexual women. Even fewer—9% of men and 6% of women—regarded most lesbians as child molesters.

Consistent with these findings, Gallup Polls have found that an increasing number of Americans would allow gay people to be elementary school teachers. For example, the proportion was 54% in 1999, compared to 27% in 1977.

Examining the Research

Even though most Americans don't regard gay people as child molesters, confusion remains widespread in this area. To understand the facts, it is important to examine the results of scientific research. However, when we evaluate research on child molestation, our task is complicated by several problems.

One problem is that we do not know to what extent the samples used in research studies are representative of all child molesters. Most studies in this area have been conducted only with convicted perpetrators or with pedophiles who sought professional help. Consequently, they may not accurately describe child molesters who have never been caught or have not sought treatment.

Terminology

A second problem is that the terminology used in this area is often confusing and can even be misleading. We can begin to address that problem by defining some basic terms.

Pedophilia and *child molestation* are used in a variety of ways, even by professionals. Pedophilia usually refers to an adult psychosexual disorder characterized by a preference for prepubescent children as sexual partners; this preference may or may not be acted upon. The term *hebephilia* is sometimes used to describe adult sexual attractions to adolescents and children who have reached puberty.

Whereas pedophilia and hebephilia refer to psychological propensities, child molestation and *child sexual abuse* are used to describe actual sexual contact between an adult and someone who has not reached the legal age of consent. In this context, someone who has not reached the age of consent is referred to as a *child*, even though he or she may be a teenager.

Although the terms are not always used consistently, it is useful to distinguish between pedophiles/hebephiles and child molesters/abusers. Pedophilia and hebephilia are diagnostic labels. Not all pedophiles and hebephiles actually molest children; an adult can be attracted to children or adolescents without ever actually engaging in sexual contact with them.

Child molestation and child sexual abuse refer to actions, and don't imply a particular psychological makeup or motive on the part of the perpetrator. Not all incidents of child sexual abuse are perpetrated by pedophiles or hebephiles; in some cases, the perpetrator has other motives for his or her actions and does not manifest an ongoing pattern of sexual attraction to children.

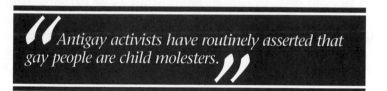

Antigay activists have routinely asserted that gay people are child molesters.

Thus, not all child sexual abuse is perpetrated by pedophiles (or hebephiles) and not all pedophiles and hebephiles actually commit abuse. Consequently, it is important to choose one's terms carefully.

Another problem related to terminology arises because sexual abuse of male children by adult men is often referred to as "homosexual molestation." The adjective "homosexual" (or "heterosexual" when a man abuses a female child) refers to the victim's gender in relation to that of the perpetrator. Unfortunately, people sometimes mistakenly interpret it as referring to the perpetrator's sexual orientation.

To avoid this confusion, it is preferable to refer to men's sexual abuse of boys with the more accurate label of *male-male* molestation. Similarly, it is preferable to refer to men's abuse of girls as *male-female* molestation. These labels are more accurate because they describe the sex of the individuals involved but don't convey implicit assumptions about the perpetrator's sexual orientation.

Typologies of Offenders

The distinction between gender of victim and sexual orientation of perpetrator is important because many child molesters don't really have an adult sexual orientation. They have never developed the capacity for mature sexual relationships with other adults, either men or women.

Over the years, this fact has been incorporated into various schemes for categorizing child molesters. For example, [David] Finkelhor and [S.] Araji (1986) proposed that perpetrators' sexual attractions should be conceptualized as ranging along a continuum with exclusive interest in children at one extreme, and exclusive interest in adult partners at the other end.

Typologies of offenders have often included a distinction between those with an enduring primary preference for children as sexual partners and those who have established age-appropriate relationships but who become sexually involved with children under unusual circumstances of extreme stress. Perpetrators in the first category—those with a more or less exclusive interest in children—have often been labeled *fixated.* Fixation means "a temporary or permanent arrestment of psychological maturation resulting from unresolved formative issues which persist and underlie the organization of subsequent phases of development." Many clinicians view fixated offenders as being "stuck" at an early stage of psychological development.

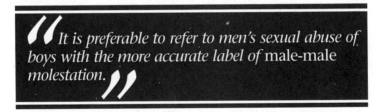

It is preferable to refer to men's sexual abuse of boys with the more accurate label of male-male molestation.

By contrast, other molesters are described as *regressed.* Regression is "a temporary or permanent appearance of primitive behavior after more mature forms of expression had been attained, regardless of whether the immature behavior was actually manifested earlier in the individual's development." Regressed offenders have developed an adult sexual orientation but under certain conditions (such as extreme stress) they return to an earlier, less mature psychological state and engage in sexual contact with children.

Some typologies of child molesters break the fixation-regression distinction into multiple categories, and some include additional categories as well. For the present discussion, the important point is that many child molesters cannot be meaningfully described as homosexuals, heterosexuals, or bisexuals because they are not really capable of a relationship with an adult man or woman. Instead of gender, their sexual attractions are based primarily on *age*. These individuals—who are often characterized as fixated—are attracted to children, not to men or women.

Using the fixated-regressed distinction, [A. Nicholas] Groth and [H.J.] Birnbaum studied 175 adult males who were convicted in Massachusetts of sexual assault against a child. None of the men had an exclusively homosexual adult sexual orientation. 83 (47%) were classified as "fixated"; 70 others (40%) were classified as regressed adult heterosexuals; the remaining 22 (13%) were classified as regressed adult bisexuals. Of the last group, Groth and Birnbaum observed that "in their adult relationships they engaged in sex on occasion with men as well as with women. However, in no case did this attraction to men *exceed* their preference for women. . . . There were no men who were primarily sexually attracted to other adult males. . . ."

Other Approaches

Other researchers have taken different approaches, but have similarly failed to find a connection between homosexuality and child molestation. Dr. Carole Jenny reviewed 352 medical charts, representing all of the sexually abused children seen in the emergency room or child abuse clinic of a Denver children's hospital during a one-year period (from July 1, 1991 to June 30, 1992). The molester was a gay or lesbian adult in only 2 of the 269 cases in which an adult molester could be identified—fewer than 1%.

In yet another approach to studying adult sexual attraction to children, some Canadian researchers observed how homosexual and heterosexual adult men responded to slides of males and females of various ages (child, pubescent, and mature adult). All of the research subjects were first screened to ensure that they preferred physically mature sexual partners. In some of the slides shown to subjects, the model was clothed; in others, he or she was nude. The slides were accompanied by audio recordings. The recordings paired with the nude models described an imaginary sexual interaction between the model and the subject. The recordings paired with the pictures of clothed models described the model engaging in neutral activities (e.g., swimming). To measure sexual arousal, changes in the subjects' penis volume were monitored while they watched the slides and listened to the audiotapes. The researchers found that homosexual males responded no more to male children than heterosexual males responded to female children.

Science cannot prove a negative. Thus, these studies do not prove that homosexual or bisexual males are no more likely than heterosexual males to molest children. However, each of them failed to prove the alternative hypothesis that homosexual males are more likely than heterosexual men to molest children or to be sexually attracted to children or adolescents.

Homosexual Men Do Not Pose a Threat

Reflecting the results of these and other studies, the mainstream view among researchers and professionals who work in the area of child sexual abuse is that homosexual and bisexual men do not pose any special threat to children. For example, in one review of the scientific literature, noted authority Dr. A. Nicholas Groth wrote:

> *Are homosexual adults in general sexually attracted to children and are preadolescent children at greater risk of molestation from homosexual adults than from heterosexual adults? There is no reason to believe so. The research to date all points to there being no significant relationship between a homosexual lifestyle and child molestation. There appears to be practically no reportage of sexual molestation of girls by lesbian adults, and the adult male who sexually molests young boys is not likely to be homosexual.*

In a more recent literature review, Dr. Nathaniel Mc-Conaghy similarly cautioned against confusing homosexuality with pedophilia. He noted, "The man who offends against prepubertal or immediately postpubertal boys is typically not sexually interested in older men or in women."

Gay Men and Lesbians Can Be Trusted in Positions of Authority

In the recent scandal involving the Catholic church, some Church officials have tried to link sexual abuse with gay priests, arguing that the victims were often adolescent boys rather than small children. Here is an example where the term *pedophilia*—referring as it does to attractions to prepubescent children—can cause confusion. More broadly, such accusations against gay priests raise the question of whether gay men or lesbians should not be trusted in positions of authority where there is any possibility of sexual abuse or harassment.

Scientific research provides no evidence that homosexual people are less likely than heterosexuals to exercise good judgment and appropriate discretion in their employment settings. There are no data, for example, showing that gay men and lesbians are more likely than heterosexual men and women to sexually harass their subordinates in the workplace. Data from studies using a variety of psychological measures do not indicate that gay people are more likely than heterosexuals to possess any psychological characteristics that would make them less capable of controlling their sexual urges, refraining from the abuse of power, obeying rules and laws, interacting effectively with others, or exercising good judgment in handling authority. . . . Sexual orientation is *not* a mental illness nor is it inherently associated with impaired psychological functioning.

> *Many child molesters cannot be meaningfully described as homosexuals, heterosexuals, or bisexuals because they are not really capable of a relationship with an adult.*

Gay men and lesbians function effectively in a wide variety of employment settings. No differences have been reported between heterosexuals, bisexuals, and homosexuals in job performance or ability to properly exercise authority in supervisory roles. As indicated by workplace policies around the United States, a large and growing number of private and public employers do not perceive a problem with hiring gay and bisexual people as employees or managers. A large number of corporations, educational institutions, and local governments have adopted policies that prohibit discrimination against employees on the basis of sexual orientation. In many cases, those organizations give employee benefits such as health insurance to employees' same-sex partners. Indeed, one reason often cited for providing such benefits is that they enable a company to remain competitive by attracting high quality employees who happen to be homosexual or bisexual.

Thus, the scientific literature does not provide any basis for organizations to avoid hiring homosexual or bisexual people, simply on the basis of their sexual orientation, for positions that involve responsibility for or supervision of others, whether children, adolescents, or adults.

There Is No Link Between Homosexuality and Pedophilia

One individual has claimed to have data that prove homosexuals to be child molesters at a higher rate than heterosexuals. That person is Paul Cameron. . . . Cameron's survey data are subject to so many methodological flaws as to be virtually meaningless. Even so, his assertions are often quoted by anti-gay organizations in their attempts to link homosexuality with child sexual abuse.

In a 1985 article published in *Psychological Reports*, Paul Cameron purported to review published data to answer the question, "Do those who commit homosexual acts disproportionately incorporate children into their sexual practices?" He concluded that "at least one-third of the sexual attacks upon youth are homosexual" and that "those who are bi- to homosexual are proportionately much more apt to molest youth" than are heterosexuals.

Cameron's findings are based on his assumption that all male-male molestations were committed by homosexuals. Moreover, a careful reading of Cameron's paper reveals several false statements about the literature he claimed to have reviewed.

For example, he cited the Groth and Birnbaum (1978) study mentioned previously as evidencing a 3:2 ratio of "heterosexual" (i.e., female victim) to "homosexual" (i.e., male victim) molestations, and he noted that "54% of all the molestations in this study were performed by bisexual or homosexual practitioners." However, Groth and Birnbaum reported that *none* of the men in their sample had an exclusively homosexual adult sexual orientation, and that *none* of the 22 bisexual men were more attracted to adult males than to adult females. Cameron's 54% statistic does not appear anywhere in the Groth and Birnbaum (1978) article, nor does Cameron explain its derivation.

It also is noteworthy that, although Cameron assumed that all male-male molestations were committed by homosexuals, he assumed that not all male-female molestations were committed by heterosexuals. He incorporated a "bisexual correction" into his data manipulations to increase further his estimate of the risk posed to children by homosexual/bisexual men.

In the latter half of his paper, Cameron considered whether "homosexual teachers have more frequent sexual interaction with their pupils." Based on 30 instances of sexual contact between a teacher and pupil reported in ten different sources published between 1920 and 1982, Cameron concluded that "a pupil would appear about 90 times more likely to be sexually assaulted by a homosexual practitioner"; the ratio rose to 100 times when Cameron added his bisexual correction.

This ratio is meaningless because no data were obtained concerning the actual sexual orientation of the teachers involved; as before, Cameron assumed that male-male contacts were perpetrated by homosexuals. Furthermore, Cameron's rationale for selecting particular sources appears to have been completely arbitrary. He described no systematic method for reviewing the literature, and apparently never reviewed the voluminous literature on the sexual development of children and adolescents. His final choice of sources appears to have slanted his findings toward what Cameron described as "the relative absence in the scientific literature of heterosexual teacher-pupil sexual events coupled with persistent, albeit infrequent, homosexual teacher-pupil sexual interactions."

A subsequent paper by Cameron and others [K. Proctor, W. Coburn, N. Forde, H. Larson and K. Cameron] described data collected in a door-to-door survey in seven U.S. cities and towns, and generally repeated the conclusions reached in [the 1985 article by] Cameron. As before, male-male sexual assaults were referred to as "homosexual" molestations and the perpetrators' sexual orientation apparently was not assessed. This study also suffers from severe methodological problems. . . .

In summary, the findings reported in the papers by Cameron et al. cannot be considered valid. The work is too methodologically flawed.

The empirical research does *not* show that gay or bisexual men are any more likely than heterosexual men to molest children. This is not to argue that homosexual and bisexual men never molest children. But there is no scientific basis for asserting that they are more likely than heterosexual men to do so. And, as explained above, many child molesters cannot be characterized as having an adult sexual orientation at all; they are fixated on children.

12

Child Sexual Abuse by Females Is a Growing Problem

Maura Dolan

Maura Dolan is a staff writer for the Los Angeles Times.

In the last two decades reports of women who sexually abuse children have risen considerably. However, though child sexual abuse by females is gaining recognition as a real problem, it still tends to be underreported. In addition, female offenders are less likely than their male counterparts to be prosecuted and convicted. Stereotypes of women as nurturing caregivers incapable of committing sexual abuse contribute to this phenomenon. People also commonly assume that males cannot be forced into sex against their will. In fact, they can be raped, though there are no accurate studies that show how often it happens.

There are 351 men in California locked up in a state mental hospital as sexually violent predators, prone to attack again and again.

Then there is Charlotte Mae Thrailkill.

The 43-year-old mother of two is California's only female violent sex offender, confined to a maximum-security state mental hospital after experts decided she was too dangerous for release.

Only a handful of women, including Thrailkill, have ever been confined to mental institutions under state laws that allow for civil commitments of sex criminals after they have served their prison terms.

Women Get Away with Abuse

Women are less likely than men to commit sex offenses, but they also are less likely to be reported and prosecuted. Many experts contend that women commit sex offenses far more often than is generally believed.

"It happens a lot more than gets reported, and I think part of that is due to our culture," said Steven B. Blum, a consulting psychologist to a sex offender program in Nebraska. "There are a lot of women who have sexual contact with teenage boys, and they don't get reported."

In the state's regular prison system, only 103 of the 9,746 women behind bars—1.06%—are there for sex offenses, including statutory rape and lewd acts with children. That compares with about 12,500 men, 8% of the total male prison population.

Paul Federoff, a forensic psychiatrist in Ottawa, Canada, said one of the female sex offenders he counsels is an exhibitionist. She opens her living room curtains and strips off her clothes when people pass by.

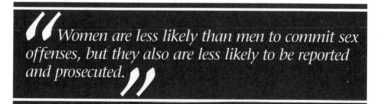

Women are less likely than men to commit sex offenses, but they also are less likely to be reported and prosecuted.

He told her that unless she stopped this illegal activity, she would be arrested.

"'Doctor, if someone calls up and says he saw me disrobing in the window, who do you think they are going arrest? Me or him?'" Federoff said she replied.

"And she is absolutely right."

It was widely assumed until recently that women just didn't sexually abuse children, Federoff said.

But during the past two decades, as parents and others have encouraged children to disclose improper sexual behavior, kids have been confiding about abuse by women as well as men.

"Now we are discovering that there are a lot of women who do sexually abuse children, but they get away with it," Federoff said. "There is a growth industry of treatment programs, particularly for adolescent female sex offenders who commit a lot of the crimes while they are baby-sitting."

Thrailkill's Story

Thrailkill, whose sexual predator status is up for review by the state in September [2002], told psychiatrists she molested children, ages 5 to 8, whom she baby-sat or enticed into her Santa Rosa apartment to play with her children. Her story, pieced together from court records, is less a rarity than crime statistics suggest.

Thrailkill, the third of six children, was born with scoliosis and a deformity in her mouth that caused speech difficulties. "She stated that school was difficult for her, not only due to her learning difficulties but also due to constant ridicule by her peers because of her physical deformities," according to a state mental heath report on file in Santa Rosa.

When older children picked on her during elementary school, "she would then bully and beat smaller, defenseless children," according to the May 2000 report.

She told counselors that she had a good relationship with her father, but complained that her mother regularly beat her with narrow leather straps, sticks and her fists. Thrailkill ran away several times between the ages of 11 and 16 and was gang-raped at age 15, she told authorities, by four men who grabbed her off a street.

That same year she was severely wounded in a random shooting and spent nine months in a hospital. She never returned to school.

Thrailkill married a U.S. Marine at 19. They had two daughters. She left him five years later, complaining their marriage was sexless, and won custody of their daughters.

Types of Female Offenders

Women who commit sex offenses often fit into one of three categories.

The "teacher-lover" or "Mrs. Robinson" type has sex with underage boys. These women fancy themselves in love with the boy and don't see the relationships as harmful, experts say.

The women tend to be immature and get an "ego boost" from the involvement, said Blum, the Nebraska psychologist, who counsels such offenders. "Without exception, all of our patients have had a substance abuse problem and also were partying with their victims," he said.

"Generally the male doesn't feel victimized," he said. "A lot of teenage boys would see that as their lucky day."

Despite such perceptions, researchers maintain that many boys may be left confused and angry, and if they are particularly young, they may be sexualized too early and have sexual problems later in life.

Women who have sex with minors make the same kinds of excuses as their male counterparts, said Florence Wolfe, co-director of Northwest Treatment Associates, a Seattle-based program for sex offenders.

Some women considered predisposed to sexually molest children are pedophiles.

Wolfe said the women tell her: "'I wanted the closeness, the excitement, not the sex. I wanted the safety. He was 13. I was only 27. The kid wanted it.'"

A study of college students and prisoners found that 16% of the college men and 46% of the male prisoners reported they had sexual experience before the age of 16 with a woman at least five years older. The average age of the men at the time of the contact was 12.

A second type of offender is called "predisposed" and includes mothers who molest their children.

Wolfe says more than 50% of the 150 female offenders she has counseled molested their own children, primarily daughters.

Some women considered predisposed to sexually molest children are pedophiles with an assortment of mental illnesses. Wolfe described one such offender she has met as a sexual sadist.

"She looks like everybody's lovable grandmother: pink cheeks, gray hair, chunky," Wolfe said. "She volunteered to baby-sit for young single moms. They jumped at the chance."

Most of this offender's victims were girls, and most were not yet verbal. The woman would slap them until their teeth cut their mouths or start a nosebleed. Their pain gave her sexual pleasure, Wolfe said.

"She finally molested a 4-year-old, and that kid was verbal

enough to tell someone," Wolfe said.

The third type of female sex criminal is called the "male-coerced" or "male-accompanied" offender. These women commit sex crimes in the company of a man. Thrailkill, who declined to be interviewed for this story, fits in this category.

Thrailkill told psychologists that she had sex with 20 to 50 different men in the year after her divorce. She eventually met Daryl Ball and allowed him and his young sons to move into her apartment in Santa Rosa. Ball introduced Thrailkill to sex with children, according to a state Mental Health Department report filed with Santa Rosa Superior Court.

Thrailkill at the time was thin, with long, dark blond hair. She looked older than her 27 years. She was quiet, shy and submissive, attorneys recall.

Seven years her senior, Ball was a brutal boyfriend, Thrailkill told others. She said he violently sodomized her, threw her from a car once and beat her to unconsciousness twice.

She molested his sons, police said. Not only was Ball aware of the molestations, he joined her in having sex with children, police and criminal records say.

Ball and Thraillkill had sex a couple of times a day with children and with as many as five children at a time, she told psychiatrists. The victims were her boyfriend's sons and other children in the apartment complex whom Thrailkill baby-sat or lured into their apartment.

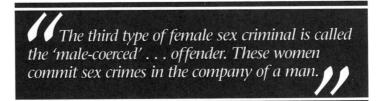

The third type of female sex criminal is called the 'male-coerced' . . . offender. These women commit sex crimes in the company of a man.

During the eight months in which she molested, Thrailkill drank and used methamphetamine, first snorting the drug and later injecting it, she told mental health workers.

"When she was intoxicated, she was sexually promiscuous, violent and sexually perverse," according to a May 2001 report by the state Department of Mental Health.

Both Thrailkill and Ball threatened the children that their parents or siblings would be killed if they told anyone. Eventually, one of the children did tell, and Thrailkill and Ball were arrested.

When a parent of one of the victims confronted Thrailkill, she said she molested because she was "afraid" of Ball, who was then 34.

"He made me do it," she said.

But in records on file at the Santa Rosa courthouse, Thrailkill admitted she molested five children—four boys and one girl—on her own. She said she abused them to get even with the victims' parents.

Thrailkill typically endured extensive mistreatment in relationships, a mental health evaluation found. When she finally felt sufficiently hurt by the abuse, she lashed out at others.

"She admits she takes anger out on weaker, often innocent individuals," a mental health counselor wrote.

Females Are Less Likely to Be Prosecuted

A 1981 national study of both reported and unreported child abuse indicated that as many as 24% of boys and 14% of girls who are molested are victimized by women.

Although sexual abuse by both men and women is underreported, female offenders are less likely than men to be prosecuted.

"I have had so many clients, both males and females, who talked about mothers or their baby-sitters molesting them," said Charlene Steen, a psychologist in Napa who has treated sex offenders for 20 years. "And they were never reported."

Dr. Robert Kolodny, who has directed behavioral research institutes and written about sexual behavior, said he periodically gets calls from befuddled prosecutors who have cases in which a man has accused a woman of rape.

"Although it sounds counterintuitive, men can indeed be raped," Kolodny said.

People commonly assume that men cannot be forced into sex against their will. But experts say men may be physically capable of sex even while under extreme duress.

Female rapists are sometimes acquaintances of their victims and get them drunk or drugged before they force them to submit to sexual acts.

"We don't really have good studies that would give us an accurate picture of how often it happens, but it is not rare . . . not a one-in-a-thousand kind of thing," Kolodny said.

Some case studies describe rapes of men committed by two or more women. In a report in the *Archives of Sexual Behavior,* two physicians described 11 cases of rapes of men, including a man who picked up a woman in a bar and then went to a motel with her.

The man had a drink and fell asleep, the 1982 report said. When he awoke, he was gagged, blindfolded and tied to the bed. He heard the voices of several women.

Steen, who is also a lawyer, described one man who was drugged and raped by two women and a man. The victim was later found wandering the streets with his clothes tied around his neck.

Observed Steen: "There are women out there who are doing some pretty horrible things."

Civil Commitment

Thrailkill initially faced more than 50 counts of felony child molesting. She pleaded no contest in 1988 to five counts of molestation in exchange for a 14-year prison sentence.

Ball, whom Thrailkill married after the arrests but divorced while in prison, pleaded no contest to several counts of lewd and lascivious conduct upon children and was sentenced to 24 years in prison.

Thraillkill began serving her sentence in September 1988 and was paroled in September 1994. She then worked in construction and had what court records described as two "normal" relationships with adult men.

In July 1996, she violated her parole by using alcohol, associating with convicted sex offenders and having contact with children.

She returned to prison and again was paroled in March 1998. Within a month, parole was revoked because she had used alcohol. The state began proceedings to commit her as a sex predator, and she did not oppose the effort.

Marie Case, a Santa Rosa criminal defense lawyer who represented her, said Thrailkill was "intimidated by the whole proceeding" and horrified that media coverage might hurt her daughters, who were then in school.

"I found her to be very shy and very private, and it was very painful for her to discuss" her past, Case said.

Thrailkill was certified as a sexually violent predator in September 1998 and sent to Patton State Hospital in San Bernardino County.

Like other sex predators who have been committed, Thrailkill's status must be reviewed by the state every two years. She may be recommitted only if two mental health experts determine her mental problems make her likely to molest again.

During therapy, she has expressed regret about her two daughters, who are now adults. Thrailkill conceded at the hospital that her daughters had been "sexual victims of her husband and emotional victims of her," a report said.

Ball, now 50, was released on parole in January [2002]. Two state-appointed mental health experts evaluated him and found he does not have a mental disorder that makes him likely to molest again.

Thrailkill is scheduled to leave Patton in September [2002] unless the state tries to renew her commitment.[1]

A staff psychologist with the department wrote that Thrailkill does not wish to be released until she is convinced she can "manage" her behavior. According to a May 2000 report, she has "genuine shame for her behavior and remorse for her victims."

"She has never shown any interest in coming out," Case said. "I think she feels safe there."

1. Charlotte Mae Thrailkill's civil commitment was renewed. As of July 2004 she is continuing her treatment at Patton State Hospital in San Bernardino County.

13

Pedophiles Use the Internet to Find Victims

Peter Wilkinson

Peter Wilkinson is a contributing editor to Rolling Stone.

Cyberspace is a virtual playground for adults seeking sex with children. The many adolescents who chat with them online fuel the pedophile's need for fantasy. However, pedophiles rarely take measures to protect their privacy and often leave a trail of evidence that will aid in their conviction. By posing as adolescents online, undercover detectives can establish relationships with pedophiles, agree to meet, and then arrest them.

For adults seeking real or imagined sex with children, Cyberspace has become an irresistible playground, offering apparent anonymity and the opportunity to meet multiple potential partners in seconds and trade pornographic photographs and short films with a couple of keystrokes. Some offenders have likened Internet chat rooms devoted to child exploitation to what a drug user might experience if provided an endless supply of crack cocaine.

And it is indeed an addiction, one that can tempt people to behave in ways they'd never thought possible. Men seeking boys spend fifteen to twenty-five hours per week online, studies show, crusty towel at the ready, cheese-stained Big Mac boxes piled around their computer, trying to meet children they would have had no access to in the offline world. Some won't leave their screens to go the bathroom. They piss in empty soda cans. . . .

The Ritual of Seduction

When [Detective] James McLaughlin logs on, posing as an underage boy, as he does most days in his comfortable office on the second floor of the Keene Police Department, he may find himself chatting with as many as eight eager adult males at a time. One recent day, McLaughlin posed as a fourteen-year-old named Brad and posted a smiling, clothed photograph of himself—in reality a photo of another officer at fourteen—as part of his user profile. Internationally, the waves of sex offenders seem to follow the sun. Earlier that morning, McLaughlin chatted with perverts from Australia and New Zealand. A new squadron of them, from Europe, logged on about 3 P.M. Eastern Standard Time.

McLaughlin "talked" "with a Texas businessman traveling in Mexico, who readily sent him a horrendous child-porn portfolio, and a middle-aged welder near Dayton, Ohio, posing as a nineteen-year-old who claimed to have performed fellatio on his twelve-year-old cousin. Each time, the chat followed a similar pattern: brief, jocular small talk suffused with flattery, followed—when a certain "trust" has been established—by the sending of child-porn images, a classic pedophile tactic designed to break down the inhibitions of boys under the age of consent. Pedophiles, by their nature, are ritualistic, likely to use the same seduction techniques over and over. In fact, for many, the seduction, and anticipation of sex, tends to be as exciting, if not more so, than sex itself. A child engaged in sex with an adult, after all, is going to be silent, as a means of resistance, not enthusiastic, as a willing partner would be.

Pedophiles, in time, also send pictures that purport to be self-portraits. "Sometimes they'll cheat with the nude pictures they send of themselves," McLaughlin says. "They'll send a picture of a penis that they've dragged off the Internet. I've got one penis eight people claim is theirs. It's like a time-share penis."

Easy to Convict

Since he started prowling the horny backrooms of the Internet, in 1996, McLaughlin has made 382 cases, many of them in New Hampshire, as well as in most other states and in fifteen foreign countries. These cases involved the arrest of men of all ages from all walks of life, including seventeen teachers, six policemen, several lawyers, a Catholic priest, a jet mechanic, a Boy Scout official and, recently, a counselor at a Massachusetts YMCA. Every one of McLaughlin's cases has resulted in a conviction, due in large part to the fact that felonious computer chat and image traffic can easily be preserved for evidentiary purposes. As McLaughlin says, "These guys become absolute evidence machines after a while." And so, as easy as it can be for child molesters to find victims on the Net, it can be just as easy to jail them—provided that law enforcement happens to be looking.

In New Hampshire, as in other states, it is a felony, punishable by three and a half to seven years in prison, to use an Internet service, such as e-mail or real-time chat, to lure or solicit a child. New Hampshire passed its law in 1999. Other states lagged behind the rapid advance of cybertechnology. Massachusetts, for one, did not pass a similar law until 2002.

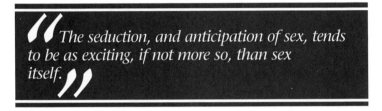

The seduction, and anticipation of sex, tends to be as exciting, if not more so, than sex itself.

The father of a college-age stepdaughter—his wife works in real estate—McLaughlin is a former Marine who started with the Keene Police Department in 1981. He began working sex-assault cases three years later, and in the Nineties, with the help of funding from the Justice Department's Internet Crimes Against Children program, developed his online specialty of tracking men interested in boys.

What drives McLaughlin can be hard to pin down. By no means does he come off as a conservative crusader. Pedophiles, notorious recidivists that they are, can and should be treated, the detective believes. Meeting victims and seeing the damage done to developing children seems to be the main source of his motivation. By virtue of the technology involved, that damage is difficult to contain. Recently, McLaughlin testified in a Georgia courtroom against a man charged with distributing child pornography, some of which he produced himself. Later, in the hall, McLaughlin ran into two boys waiting their turn to testify and immediately recognized them. He'd seen both of them naked and engaged in sexual acts that the defendant had filmed with a digital camera and distributed, without their consent, on the Internet. "That offender will no doubt be convicted," McLaughlin says wearily. "But after all is said and done, those boys' pictures will always be on the Internet.". . .

What about entrapment? The rule for cybercops like McLaughlin is this: They can't encourage potential targets to do something, to engage in a behavior that they don't already have a predisposition to engage in. On the Internet, then, if a male adult in a room titled "fourteen-year-old boys jerking off" is seeking just that, and to engage said boys in conversation, send them pornography or try to meet them, that constitutes predisposition, just by virtue of his presence and behavior. Possession of child porn, in and of itself, shows predisposition. "In fact," says McLaughlin, "we've never lost an Internet case through a successful entrapment defense."

Many pedophiles have read about McLaughlin and the operation he runs out of Keene, and some even have sent warnings about him to one another, accompanied by his picture. It doesn't seem to matter. These same men will still send child porn to marks who claim to live in Keene or in the immediate vicinity. Cyber-sex addiction easily overrules security concerns. "Their pathology is stronger than common sense," McLaughlin says. "They just say to themselves, 'I'll risk it today,' and the majority of days they're not going to get caught."

After all is said and done, those boys' pictures will always be on the Internet.

Few take even the simplest precautions. When McLaughlin seizes computers, most of them, he finds, are not password-protected, and the screen saver is a naked child or a slide show of naked children. Nor is the offender using encryption or presenting a faked service provider. "They get overwhelmed by the material and all the people engaging in the behavior," McLaughlin says. "They feel that they're a grain of sand and it's not their turn to be arrested. Less than one percent are using technology to obscure who they are."

Take josunrise2002. A link on his online profile led to a photograph of his pride and joy, a red 1974 Pontiac GTO that he drove on the street and exhibited at car shows. Only problem: The photo also clearly showed the car's Connecticut BAD 74 license plate. "It looks better in person," he informed Adam. "Kids love the thing."

Oftentimes these days, in his effort to identify the person

behind the screen name, McLaughlin doesn't even have to bother with the weeks-long process of serving a subpoena on AOL or some other Internet service provider to determine who opened a particular account. He'll simply use conversational tricks to get them to reveal their full name and address via instant message. One day not long ago, McLaughlin pulled this off after a chat that lasted only thirty-seven minutes.

Exploiting the Pedophile's Need for Fantasy

Pedophilia is a fantasy-fueled disorder. Offenders get extremely aroused during the chat, thinking about a child sitting in front of a computer in his bedroom. "If you talk to them post-ejaculation," McLaughlin says, "you can see the difference. Some have regrets about even engaging in the chat."

Sex offenders, as part of an effort to rationalize their behavior, may think of themselves as mentors, that having sex with minors isn't damaging. Rather, it's therapeutic, they make themselves believe, a way for a child to be mentored and even empowered. So McLaughlin presents himself as a fatherless boy, a naive child interested in sexual knowledge. "These guys have their arms open, willing to embrace that," he says. "They think they're being altruistic, but of course it's full of exploitation. They're not even in touch with the fact that they're really out for their needs. You take those cognitive distortions of sex offenders and use those to undermine them."

The idea, basically, is to match their fantasy.

"I'm going to tell him I don't have a father," McLaughlin says. "I'm going to tell him I have a younger brother and we share a bedroom, because I want to create a fertile ground for him to give me some guidance about how I can molest my brother, which they typically will do." Though McLaughlin can receive child porn in the course of an investigation, he can't transmit any, so when an offender asks for nude pictures of him, he'll simply say that he has some Polaroids but no way to scan them. He'll say his mom works erratic hours so he can end a chat at any moment by saying "Mom's home."

"I'm going to have a late onset of puberty, which is attractive to some sex offenders because they have more interest in a younger body," he says. "I'm going to have the kid involved in sports so he has access to locker rooms where he can see other kids. It's extremely involved. You just don't pop into a chat room. The work you do before you hit that mouse is incredible."

Asked if he is a cop, McLaughlin is within law-enforcement undercover guidelines to say no. And he has other tricks up his sleeve: "'I typically ask them first, 'Are you a police officer?' In fact, one said yes, and we ended up arresting him.

"Or I'd say, 'Yeah, I'm a police officer. You're under arrest. Get your hands away from your crotch and step away from your computer.' They'd go, 'Ha, ha, ha!' and we'd go on."

Sadly, as digital-camera prices fall to less than $100 for a very basic model, more and more children participate "on cam" in their own victimization. "I see kids eight and nine years old exposing themselves on QuickCams, an electronic you-show-me-yours, I'll-show-you-mine type of thing," he says. In cases like these, McLaughlin quietly contacts the parents, and no criminal charges are filed.

Pedophilia is a fantasy-fueled disorder.

Sometimes boys sell themselves, in a sense, online. "We did paper routes as kids," McLaughlin says. "Now, twelve-, thirteen-, fourteen-year-old kids go online and do sex shows and accept Mastercard and Visa, through PayPal, to do so. Or they can sell their soiled underwear through eBay for twenty-five dollars a shot." When McLaughlin visits these homes, he usually finds that parents had absolutely no idea what was going on in the next room.

Early in his career as a cyberhunter, McLaughlin chatted with some pedophiles for four hours a day. He has cut way back on that now and can tell in just a few minutes if a potential target is worth his time and attention. "What you have to do is watch your schedule more than any thing else. You leave this stuff here," he says, motioning to tall stacks of chat-room transcripts and sealed evidence pouches containing enema bags. "I don't go home and tell my wife I was talking to a guy eating his turds." To unwind, McLaughlin takes long daily bicycle rides and bakes blueberry pies. . . .

Making an Arrest

It's time to make a grab. A bit before 9 A.M., McLaughlin and a colleague pull their unmarked police car into the KFC parking

lot on Key Road in Keene, and wait. A fifty-six-year-old pedophile using the screen name "peterxx2" is on his way from
another town in New Hampshire to meet "Adam"—McLaughlin once again posing as a fourteen-year-old boy interested in
sex with adults.

McLaughlin met peterxx2, an operator of heavy equipment, more than a year before, in an online boy-lover club
called the Ghoul Drool, members of which also like to hold
face-to-face "offline" meetings around the country. Peterxx2
advised Adam how to stretch his anal opening using dildos and
sent Adam an enema bag, a filthy enema tube and a tub of
Vaseline, along with two pages of directions about how to give
himself an enema and achieve maximum sexual pleasure. "It
was erotic for him to think he was educating this child,"
McLaughlin says.

Though peterxx2 was careful not to send Adam any images
of child porn, he did admit that he'd sexually abused two
young boys and was targeting a new one. "What really upped
the ante for me," McLaughlin says, "was that he sent me a picture of a twelve-year-old boy, his newest boy that he was going
to seduce. I wanted to take him out before that happened.". . .

Many pedophiles are so excited and nervous about their
encounters with children that they show up hours early for
scheduled assignations. Some run counter-surveillance and
watch the meet area two or three hours ahead of time. Not pe-
terxx2, who shows up two minutes late, at 9:02, behind the
wheel of a brown Ford Ranger. He carries condoms, lube and a
camera. His clothes are filthy. McLaughlin takes him into custody without a struggle. The same day, officers in peterxx2's
hometown in New Hampshire search his house and find child
porn and, because the plumbing isn't working, a bucketful of
urine and feces.

Peterxx2 says little after his arrest, which is somewhat unusual. As horrified and embarrassed about being publicly exposed for what they are, many cyberpervs want to talk, at great
length, about their activity and their rationalizations for it. And
McLaughlin listens. "As bizarre as this sounds, I'm the first person that they've typically opened up about their life of perversion to, so somehow I become their best buddy," he says. "I get
more Christmas cards from prison than I do from my extended-
family members."

Organizations to Contact

The editors have compiled the following list of organizations concerned with the issues debated in this book. The descriptions are derived from materials provided by the organizations. All have publications or information available for interested readers. The list was compiled on the date of publication of the present volume; names, addresses, phone and fax numbers, and e-mail and Internet addresses may change. Be aware that many organizations take several weeks or longer to respond to inquiries, so allow as much time as possible.

ACT for Kids
210 W. Sprague, Spokane, WA 99201
(866) 348-5437 • fax: (509) 747-0609
e-mail: resources@actforkids.org • Web site: www.actforkids.org

ACT for Kids is a nonprofit organization that provides resources, consultation, research, and training for the prevention and treatment of child abuse and sexual violence. The organization publishes workbooks, manuals, and books such as *He Told Me Not to Tell* and *How to Survive the Sexual Abuse of Your Child*.

American Academy of Child and Adolescent Psychiatry (AACAP)
3615 Wisconsin Ave. NW, Washington, DC 20016-3007
(202) 966-7300 • fax: (202) 966-2891
Web site: www.aacap.org

AACAP is a nonprofit organization that supports and advances child and adolescent psychiatry through research and the distribution of information. The academy's goal is to provide information that will remove the stigma associated with mental illnesses and assure proper treatment for children who suffer from mental or behavioral disorders due to child abuse, molestation, or other factors. AACAP publishes "Facts for Families" on a variety of issues concerning disorders that may affect children and adolescents. Titles include "Child Sexual Abuse" and "Responding to Child Sexual Abuse."

American Bar Association (ABA)
Center on Children and the Law
740 Fifteenth St. NW, Washington, DC 20005
(202) 662-1720 • fax: (202) 662-1755
e-mail: ctrchildlaw@abanet.org
Web site: www.abanet.org/child/home.html

The ABA Center for Children and the Law aims to improve the quality of life for children through advances in law and public policy. It publishes the monthly *ABA Juvenile and Child Welfare Law Reporter* and specializes in providing information on legal matters related to the protection of children.

American Professional Society on the Abuse of Children (APSAC)
940 NE Thirteenth St., TCH 3B 3406, Oklahoma City, OK 73104
(405) 271-8202 • fax: (405) 271-2931
e-mail: john-madden@ouhsc.edu • Web site: www.apsac.org

APSAC is dedicated to improving the coordination of services in the fields of child abuse prevention, treatment, and research. It publishes a quarterly newsletter, the *Advisor,* and the *Journal of Interpersonal Violence.*

Association for the Treatment of Sexual Abuse (ATSA)
4900 SW Griffith Dr., Suite 274, Beaverton, OR 97005
(503) 643-1023 • fax: (503) 643-5084
e-mail: atsa@atsa.com • Web site: www.atsa.com

To eliminate sexual victimization and protect communities from sex offenders, ATSA fosters research, furthers professional education, and advances professional standards and practices in the field of sex offender evaluation and treatment. The association publishes the quarterly *ATSA Journal.*

Canadian Society for the Investigation of Child Abuse (CSICA)
PO Box 42066, Acadia Postal Outlet, Calgary, AB T2J 7A6 Canada
(403) 289-8385
e-mail: info@csica.zener.com • Web site: www.csica.zener.com

CSICA is a nonprofit society formed to provide a coordinated, professional approach to child sexual abuse investigations. The society presents seminars and workshops on child sexual abuse and trains investigators. CSICA responds to the needs of abused children. By teaching children about the courtroom and court processes, CSICA's programs enhance the judicial process and reduce the emotional trauma experienced by children in delivering their testimony in court. On its Web site CSICA provides access to court preparation training materials and a children's video and comic book, *You're Not Alone,* in which children share their courtroom experiences.

Center for Sex Offender Management
8403 Colesville Rd., Suite 720, Silver Spring, MD 20910
(301) 589-9383 • fax: (301) 589-3505
e-mail: cartermm@cepp.com • Web site: www.csom.org

The Center for Sex Offender Management, which is sponsored by the U.S. Justice Department, supports state and local jurisdictions in the effective management of sex offenders under community supervision. Their goal is to improve public safety by preventing further victimization. The center provides technical training and assistance to professionals in the field of sex offender management. Publications include documents on community education, community notification, sex offender registration, victim advocacy, and more.

Child Welfare League of America (CWLA)
440 First St. NW, 3rd Fl., Washington, DC 20001-2085
(202) 638-2952 • fax: (202) 638-4004
Web site: www.cwla.org

The Child Welfare League of America is an association of more than seven hundred public and private agencies and organizations devoted to improving the lives of children. CWLA publications include the book *Tender Mercies: Inside the World of a Child Abuse Investigator,* the quarterly magazine *Children's Voice,* and the bimonthly journal *Child Welfare.*

FaithTrust Institute
2400 N. Forty-fifth St., #10, Seattle, WA 98103
(206) 634-1903 • fax: (206) 634-0115
e-mail: info@faithtrustinstitute.org
Web site: www.faithtrustinstitute.org

The center serves as an interreligious educational resource addressing issues of sexual and domestic violence. The goal of the FaithTrust Institute is to assist religious leaders in the task of ending abuse. The center publishes books and videos on sexual abuse by clergy, and *Working Together,* a quarterly newsletter that includes articles, editorials, book reviews, resources, and information about local, national, and international prevention efforts.

Family Research Laboratory (FRL)
University of New Hampshire, Durham, NH 03824-3586
(603) 862-1888 • fax: (603) 862-1122
e-mail: doreen.cole@unh.edu • Web site: www.unh.edu/frl

The FRL is an independent research group that studies the causes and consequences of family violence, including physical and sexual abuse of children, and the connections between family violence and other social problems. A bibliography of works on these subjects, produced by staff members under the sponsorship of the University of New Hampshire, is available from the FRL.

Kempe Children's Center
1825 Marion St., Denver, CO 80218
(303) 864-5300 • fax: (303) 864-5302
e-mail: kempe@kempecenter.org • Web site: www.kempecenter.org

The Kempe Children's Center, formerly the C. Henry Kempe National Center for the Prevention and Treatment of Child Abuse and Neglect, is a resource for research on all forms of child abuse and neglect. It is committed to multidisciplinary approaches to improve recognition, treatment, and prevention of abuse. The center's resource library offers a catalog of books, booklets, information packets, and articles on child sexual abuse issues.

Klaas Kids Foundation
PO Box 925, Sausalito, CA 94966
(415) 331-6867 • fax: (415) 331-5633
e-mail: klaaskids@pacbell.net • Web site: www.klaaskids.org

The Klaas Kids Foundation was established in 1994 after the death of twelve-year-old kidnap-and-murder victim Polly Hannah Klaas. The foundation's goal is to acknowledge that crimes against children deserve a high priority and form partnerships with concerned citizens, the private sector, organizations, law enforcement, and legislators to fight crimes against children. The foundation publishes a quarterly newsletter, the *Klaas Action Review*.

Legal Momentum
395 Hudson St., New York, NY 10014
(212) 925-6635 • fax: (212) 226-1066
e-mail: peo@legalmomentum.org
Web site: www.legalmomentum.org

Legal Momentum, formerly NOW Legal Defense and Education Fund, is a branch of the National Organization for Women, an organization that seeks to end discrimination against women. Legal Momentum offers a publications list and a legal resources kit on incest and child sexual abuse.

The Linkup
PO Box 429, Pewee Valley, KY 40056
(502) 241-5544 • fax: (502) 290-4056
e-mail: director@thelinkup.org • Web site: www.thelinkup.org

The primary goal of the Linkup is to prevent clergy abuse and to empower and assist its victims to overcome its traumatic effects on their lives. The Linkup also encourages religious institutions to develop and implement responsible, accountable policies and procedures. On its Web site, the Missing Link Online, the Linkup publishes news and articles.

Male Survivor
5505 Connecticut Ave. NW, Washington, DC 20015-2601
(800) 738-4181
Web site: www.malesurvivor.org

Male Survivor, formerly National Organization on Male Sexual Victimization (NOMSV), seeks to prevent abused boys from becoming self-destructive or abusive adolescents and men. Male Survivor also helps the public to recognize and understand males who have been sexually abused and promotes action to confront and fight male sexual abuse. The Male Survivor Web site provides information for survivors, clinicians, and caregivers. The organization publishes a quarterly newsletter, *Male Survivor*.

National Center for Missing and Exploited Children (NCMEC)
699 Prince St., Alexandria, VA 22314-3175
(703) 739-0321 • (800) THE LOST • fax: (703) 274-2200
Web site: www.missingkids.com

The NCMEC serves as a clearinghouse of information on missing and exploited children and coordinates child protection efforts with the private sector. A number of publications on these issues are available, including guidelines for parents whose children are testifying in court, help for abused children, and booklets such as *Child Molesters: A Behavioral Analysis* and *How to Keep Your Child Safe: A Message to Every Parent*.

National Center for Prosecution of Child Abuse
American Prosecutors Research Institute
99 Canal Center Plaza, Suite 510, Alexandria, VA 22314
(703) 549-4253 • fax: (703) 836-3195
e-mail: ncpca@ndaa-apri.org
Web site: www.ndaa-apri.org/apri/programs/ncpca/ncpca-home.html

The center seeks to improve the investigation and prosecution of child abuse cases. A clearinghouse on child abuse laws and court reforms, the center supports research on reducing courtroom trauma for child victims. It publishes a monthly newsletter, _Update_, as well as monographs, bibliographies, special reports, and a manual for prosecutors, _Investigation and Prosecution of Child Abuse._

National Clearinghouse on Child Abuse and Neglect Information
330 C St. SW, Washington, DC 20447
(703) 385-7565 • (800) 394-3366 • fax: (703) 385-3206
e-mail: nccanch@calib.com • Web site: http://nccanch.acf.hhs.gov

This national clearinghouse collects, catalogs, and disseminates information on all aspects of child maltreatment, including identification, prevention, treatment, public awareness, training, and education. The clearinghouse offers various reports, fact sheets, and bulletins concerning child abuse and neglect.

National Criminal Justice Reference Service (NCJRS)
PO Box 6000, Rockville, MD 20849
(800) 851-3420 • (301) 519-5212
Web site: www.ncjrs.org

The NCJRS is a primary source of information on crime victims as well as research and statistics on child abuse. It distributes a child abuse information package and several pamphlets, such as _Child Sexual Abuse Victims and Their Treatment_ and _Police and Child Abuse._

National Institute of Justice (NIJ)
810 Seventh St. NW, Washington, DC 20531
(202) 307-2942 • fax: (202) 307-6394
Web site: ojp.usdoj.gov/nij

The NIJ is the research and development agency of the U.S. Department of Justice, established to prevent and reduce crime and to improve the criminal justice system. Among its publications is the report _When the Victim Is a Child_, which reviews research on the consequences of child sexual abuse and the capabilities of children as witnesses.

The Safer Society Foundation
PO Box 340, Brandon, VT 05733-0340
(802) 247-3132 • fax: (802) 247-4233
Web site: www.safersociety.org

The Safer Society Foundation is a national research, advocacy, and referral center for the prevention of sexual abuse of children and adults. The Safer Society Press publishes studies and books on the prevention of sexual abuse and on treatment for sexual abuse victims and offenders, including _Back on Track: Boys Dealing with Sexual Abuse._

Sexcriminals.com
Web site: www.sexcriminals.com

The goal of sexcriminals.com is to serve visitors by providing information, resources, and support for those concerned about or affected by sex crimes. The site hosts discussion forums that allow users to share experiences, ask questions, receive support, and debate related topics.

Links to state and local sex offender registries are available. The site also has an extensive news archive with a comprehensive list of topics related to child sexual abuse.

Sex Information and Education Council of the United States (SIECUS)
130 W. Forty-second St., Suite 350, New York, NY 10036-7802
(212) 819-9770 • fax: (212) 819-9776
e-mail: siecus@siecus.org • Web site: www.siecus.org

SIECUS is a clearinghouse for information on sexuality, with a special interest in sex education. It publishes sex education curricula, the bimonthly newsletter *SIECUS Report*, and fact sheets on sex education issues. Its articles, bibliographies, and book reviews often address the role of education in identifying, reducing, and preventing sexual abuse.

Stop It Now!
PO Box 495, Haydenville, MA 01039
(413) 268-3096 • (888) PREVENT
e-mail: info@stopitnow.org • Web site: www.stopitnow.org

Stop It Now! is a nonprofit organization with the vision of helping to end the sexual abuse of children. Its mission is to motivate all abusers and potential abusers to stop and seek help. Stop It Now! also works to educate other adults about the ways to stop sexual abuse. Its publications include *Working Upstream: A Public Health Approach to Preventing the Sexual Abuse of Children* and *Talking with Your Children About Child Sexual Abuse*.

Survivors Network of Those Abused by Priests (SNAP)
PO Box 6416, Chicago, IL 60680-6416
(877) 762-7432
Web site: www.survivorsnetwork.org

SNAP provides support for men and women who have been sexually abused by any clergy, including priests, brothers, nuns, deacons, and teachers. The network provides an extensive phone network, advocacy, information, and referrals. SNAP's Web site provides access to stories, statements, and speeches from survivors; a discussion board; news; and information on legal issues.

Voice of the Faithful (VOTF)
PO Box 423, Newton Upper Falls, MA 02464
(617) 558-5252
Web site: www.votf.org

VOTF is a lay group formed in response to the 2002 clergy sexual abuse crisis with the aim of restoring trust between the Catholic laity and hierarchy and rebuilding the Catholic Church. The organization supports survivors and "priests of integrity" and promotes church reform. The VOTF Web site provides access to survivor and clergy support services and articles on the child sexual abuse crisis.

Bibliography

Books

Paul R. Abramson — *A House Divided: Suspicions of Mother-Daughter Incest (Based on a True Story)*. New York: Norton, 2001.

Devon B. Adams — *Summary of State Sex Offender Registries*. Washington, DC: U.S. Department of Justice, Office of Justice Programs, Bureau of Justice Statistics, 2002.

Leigh Baker — *Protecting Your Children from Sexual Predators*. New York: St. Martin's, 2002.

Kevin Bales — *Disposable People: New Slavery in the Global Economy*. Berkeley and Los Angeles: University of California Press, 1999.

David Race Bannon — *Race Against Evil: The Secret Missions of the Interpol Agent Who Tracked the World's Most Sinister Criminals: A Real-Life Drama*. Far Hills, NJ: New Horizons, 2003.

Kathryn Brohl — *When Your Child Has Been Molested: A Parents' Guide to Healing and Recovery*. San Francisco: Jossey-Bass, 2004.

Amitai Etzioni — *The Limits of Privacy*. New York: Basic Books, 1999.

Linda Lee Foltz — *Kids Helping Kids Break the Silence of Sexual Abuse*. Pittsburgh: Lighthouse Point, 2003.

David France — *Our Fathers: The Secret Life of the Catholic Church in an Age of Scandal*. New York: Broadway, 2004.

Amy Hammel-Zabin — *Conversations with a Pedophile: In the Interest of Our Children*. Fort Lee, NJ: Barricade, 2003.

Judith Levine — *Harmful to Minors: The Perils of Protecting Children from Sex*. Minneapolis: University of Minnesota Press, 2002.

Stephen G. Michaud — *The Evil That Men Do: FBI Profiler Roy Hazelwood's Journey into the Minds of Sexual Predators*. New York: St. Martin's, 1999.

Jan Morrison — *A Safe Place: A Guidebook for Living Beyond Sexual Abuse*. Colorado Springs, CO: Waterbrook, 2002.

Dorothy Rabinowitz — *No Crueler Tyrannies: Accusations, False Witness, and Other Terrors of Our Times*. New York: Simon & Schuster, 2003.

Donna Rafanello   *Can't Touch My Soul: A Guide for Lesbian Survivors of Child Sexual Abuse.* Los Angeles: Alyson, 2004.

Sue Righthand   *Juveniles Who Sexually Offend: A Review of the Professional Literature.* Washington, DC: Office of Juvenile Justice and Delinquency Prevention, 2001.

Lori S. Robinson   *I Will Survive: The African-American Guide to Healing from Sexual Assault and Abuse.* New York: Seal, 2003.

Anna C. Salter   *Predators: Pedophiles, Rapists, and Other Sex Offenders: Who They Are, How They Operate, and How We Can Protect Ourselves and Our Children.* New York: Basic Books, 2003.

Christiane Sanderson   *The Seduction of Children: Empowering Parents and Teachers to Protect Children from Child Sexual Abuse.* New York: Jessica Kingsley, 2004.

A.W. Richard Sipe   *Celibacy in Crisis: A Secret World Revisited.* New York: Brunner-Routledge, 2003.

Holly A. Smith   *Fire of the Five Hearts: A Memoir of Treating Incest.* New York: Brunner-Routledge, 2002.

Robin D. Stone   *No Secrets, No Lies: How Black Families Can Heal from Sexual Abuse.* New York: Broadway, 2004.

Max Taylor and Ethel Quayle   *Child Pornography: An Internet Crime.* New York: Brunner-Routledge, 2003.

Pnina Tobin   *Keeping Kids Safe: A Child Sexual Abuse Prevention Manual.* Alameda, CA: Hunter House, 2002.

Periodicals

Jeffrey Bartholet   "The Web's Dark Secret," *Newsweek*, March 19, 2001.

Sandra G. Boodman   "How Deep the Scars of Abuse? Some Victims Crippled; Others Stay Resilient," *Washington Post*, July 29, 2002.

Tom Chiarella   "My Education," *Esquire*, May 2003.

John Cloud   "Pedophilia," *Time*, April 29, 2002.

Kevin Culligan   "Sacred Rage and Rebuilding the Church: Jesus Shows How Emotions Can Move Us to Action," *National Catholic Reporter*, September 13, 2002.

Theodore Dalrymple   "Our Great Societal Neverland," *National Review*, December 22, 2003.

Judy Dutton   "Why She Slept with Her Student," *Redbook*, August 2002.

Catherine Edwards   "Sex-Slave Trade Is Thriving," *Insight on the News*, August 13, 2001.

Marilyn Elias	"Gays and the Catholic Church Sex Abuse Crisis," *USA Today*, July 16, 2002.
Annette Foglino	"Teachers Who Prey on Kids: Why They're Still Going Free," *Good Housekeeping*, December 1, 2003.
David France	"Confessions of a Fallen Priest," *Newsweek*, April 1, 2002.
Bill Hewitt	"Breaking the Silence: Often Shamed and Ignored, Victims of Sexual Abuse by Priests Are Speaking Out, Putting Pressure on the Catholic Church to Confront the Problem Once and for All," *People Weekly*, April 1, 2002.
Toni Cavanagh Johnson	"Sexualized Children and Children Who Molest," *SIECUS Report*, October/November 2000.
Tamara Jones	"The Predator in the Classroom: It's Called 'Pass the Trash,'" *Good Housekeeping*, May 2003.
Linda Marsa	"Treat the Abuser, Reduce the Risk?" *Los Angeles Times*, May 13, 2002.
Liza Mundy	"America's Dirty Little Secret," *Redbook*, September 2001.
Warren Richey	"Megan's Law Faces High-Court Test," *Christian Science Monitor*, November 13, 2002.
Kit R. Roane	"The Long Arm of Abuse," *U.S. News & World Report*, May 6, 2002.
Stephen J. Rossetti	"The Catholic Church and Child Sexual Abuse: Distortions, Complexities and Resolutions," *America*, April 22, 2002.
Jessica Snyder Sachs	"Preventing the Unthinkable: Are You Doing All You Can to Protect Your Child from Sexual Abuse?" *Parenting*, October 1, 2003.
Allen Salkin	"'My Female Pastor Molested Me,'" *Cosmopolitan*, August, 2002.
Brandon Spun	"Closed Doors and Childhoods Lost," *Insight on the News*, January 28, 2002.
Richard E. Vatz	"Sexual Predator Statutes and Psychiatric Confusion," *USA Today Magazine*, July 2001.
Wendy Murray Zoba	"The Hidden Slavery," *Christianity Today*, November 2003.

Index

Allen, Michael, 58
American Association of University
   Women (AAUW) Educational
   Foundation, 18
*American Journal of Law and
   Medicine,* 59
Archives of Sexual Behavior
   (journal), 79–81, 84, 101
Ashcroft, John, 41
Ausherman, Christopher Lee, 66

Ball, Daryl, 100–101, 102
Behavior Research and Therapy
   (journal), 80
Berlin, Fred, 61
Beyond Tolerance (Jenkins), 36
Birnbaum, H.J., 91, 94
Blum, Steven B., 97, 98–99
Blumenthal, Richard, 8
Bryant, Anita, 87

Cameron, K., 95
Cameron, Paul, 94, 95
celibacy, priest sexual abuse and,
   26, 27
Census, U.S., 78–79
child molestation, terminology of,
   88–89
child pornography, Internet
   is rarely punished, 36–37
   law enforcement responses to,
      42–43
child protective services (CPS), 11
child sexual abuse
   child prostitution as, 51–53
   homosexual, consequences of,
      84–85
   homosexuality and
      link has not been shown,
         91–92, 94–95
      opinions on link between,
         87–88
   is underreported, 9, 97
   in schools, 20–21
   substantiated, decline in, 11
      evidence for, 12–14
   see also prevention/intervention
      efforts

Christensen, Scott, 41, 48
civil commitment, 54, 66–67
   application of, to nonpredators,
      58–60
   of female sexual offenders,
      96–97, 102–103
   mental health and, 56–58
   violate civil rights, 55–56
Clinton, Bill, 7
Coburn, W., 95
*Connecticut Department of Public
   Safety v. Doe* (2003), 8, 71
Constitution, U.S. *See* Due Process
   clause
convictions, for child abuse, 9
Curl, Tom, 48
Curran, J. Joseph, 68

Dailey, Timothy J., 77
Demography (journal), 79
Department of Education, U.S.,
   19–20
Department of Justice, U.S., 42
Dolan, Maura, 96
drugs, in treatment of sexual
   predators, 62
Due Process clause
   importance of, 63
   predator laws violate, 55–56
      con, 74–75

Eberstadt, Mary, 83
Education Week (journal), 21
"Educator Sexual Misconduct"
   (American Association of
   University Women Educational
   Foundation), 19

Falk, Adam, 59
Family Planning Perspectives
   (journal), 79
Family Research Council, 78
Federal Bureau of Investigation
   (FBI), 42, 46–48
Federoff, Paul, 97–98
Finkelhor, David, 11, 84, 90
fixation, 90
Forde, N., 95

Foucha, Terry, 57
Foucha v. Louisiana (1992), 57–58
Fourteenth Amendment. *See* Due
  Process clause
Freund, Kurt, 79
Frontain, Raymond-Jean, 82

Gallup Poll, 88
Garcia, Michael, 41
Gardner, Steven Allen, 43
*Gay Canon: Great Books Every Gay
  Man Should Read, The*
  (anthology), 83
Gay Community News (newspaper),
  81–82
Gay Report, The (Jay and Young),
  80
General Social Survey, 78
Ginsberg, Allen, 82
Grosfeld, Sharon, 67
Groth, A. Nicholas, 91, 92, 94

Hanson, Karl, 61
Harris, Kamala, 51
hebephilia, 88
Hecht, Sue, 66
Hendrie, Caroline, 17
Herek, Gregory M., 86
*History of Gay Literature: The Male
  Tradition, A* (anthology), 83
homosexuality
  pedophilia and
    in gay culture, 81–84
    link has not been shown,
      91–92, 94–95
    opinions on link between,
      87–88
  priest sexual abuse and, 26–27
"Homosexuality and Child Sexual
  Abuse" (Family Research
  Council), 78
Horaling, Norma, 52
"Hostile Hallways II" (American
  Association of University
  Women), 21
Houston Law Review, 59

Immigration and Customs
  Enforcement Agency (ICE), 42,
  45–46
International Crimes Against
  Children initiative, 48
*International Journal of Offender
  Therapy and Comparative
  Criminology*, 81

Internet
  child pornography on, 35–36
    is rarely punished, 36–37
    law enforcement efforts to
      prevent, 46–49
  pedophiles' use of, 47
    arrest for, 110
    convictions for, 105–106
    sexual addiction and, 107
    undercover surveillance of, 105
Internet Crimes Against Children
  Task Forces, 42, 49
involuntary commitment. *See* civil
  commitment laws
Isaac, Katie, 59

Jackson, Kristen, 70–71, 76
Jackson, Mark, 70, 76
Jackson, Sharon, 70, 76
Janus, Eric, 58
Jay, Karla, 80
Jenkins, Philip, 35
Jenny, Carole, 91
John Jay College, 30
John Paul II (pope), 24
Jones, Lisa M., 11
Journal of Child Psychiatry, 78
Journal of Interpersonal Violence, 81
Journal of Sex Research, 79
*Journal of the American Medical
  Association*, 84

Kanka, Megan Nicole, 7
Kanka, Richard, 8
Kansas v. Hendricks (1997), 55, 57,
  59, 63
Kepner, Jim, 82
Kesey, Ken, 60
Klein, Alisa, 9
Kolodny, Robert, 101
Krafft-Ebing, Richard von, 81

Larson, H., 95
Lawler, Gregory, 20
LeDuc, Daniel, 64
Longo, Robert E., 9
Lourdeau, Keith, 41, 46
Lyons, Katherine, 18

Martinac, Paul, 83–84
Matson, Scott, 67
McConaghy, Nathaniel, 92
McHarry, Mark, 54
McLaughlin, James, 105–10
Megan's Law, 7–10

constitutionality of, 71–75
has been effective, 72
see also civil commitment laws
Mertz, Carlin, 20
Minnesota Student Survey, 13
Montgomery, Lori, 64
Moral Panic (Jenkins), 37
Morrison, Jimmy Richard, 43

National Crime Victimization
Survey (NCVS), 12, 13
National Health and Social Life
Survey, 78
National Review Board for the
Protection of Children and
Young People, 23
National Survey of Men, 79
No Child Left Behind Act (2002),
17, 19
North American Man-Boy Love
Association (NAMBLA), 82

offenders
characteristics of, 78, 90–91
priest sexual abusers, 30–31
sexual abusers on Internet, 105
female
underreporting/prosecution of,
97, 101–102
types of, 98–101
polygraph testing of, 66
satellite tracking of, 65–66, 67–68
One Flew Over the Cuckoo's Nest
(Kesey), 60
Operation Peerless, 48–49
Operation Peer Pressure, 47
Operation Peer Pursuit, 45
Operation Predator, 45–46

pedophiles
homosexual, are overrepresented
in child sexual abuse cases, 79
use of Internet by, 47
arrest of, 110
convictions of, 105–106
sexual addiction and, 107
undercover surveillance of, 105
women as, 99–100
pedophilia
fantasy and, 108–10
vs. hebephilia, 88–89
among priests, 32

peer-to-peer (P2P) computer
networks, child pornography

traded on, 42, 44
FBI actions against, 46–48
prevention/intervention efforts
for child prostitution, 52–53
as factor in decline in reported
cases, 13
for priest sexual abuse, 29–30
for sexual predators, 62–63
priests, sexual abuse by
characteristics of accused, 30–31
church policies addressing, 25
failure of bishops to respond to,
27–28
link with pedophilia vs.
homosexuality, 92–93
prevalence of, 18
recommendations to prevent,
28–29
responses to allegations of, 32–33
time period for, 33–34
victims of, 31–32
privacy, vs. public safety, 7–8
Proctor, K., 95
prostitution, child
children are victimized by laws
on, 50–51
interventions for, 52–53
as sexual abuse, 51–53
PROTECT Act (2003), 44
Psalm 32, 34
Psychological Reports (journal), 94
public awareness, 14–15
of child pornography problem,
39–40
community notification
increases, 9–10

Rapid Risk Assessment for Sexual
Offender Recidivism (RRASOR),
61
recidivism
cannot be predicted, 75–76
risk assessment of, 61
regression, 90
reporting, of child sexual abuse, 9
by female abusers, 15–16
reasons for decline in, 12
research, 15–16
on child pornography, 38–39
on gay pedophilia, problems
with, 88, 94–95
on sexual abuse in schools, No
Child Left Behind Act and
mandate for, 19–20
"Revisiting Megan's Law and Sex

Offender Registration" (Longo), 9
Rosenblatt, Richard B., 67
Ryan, Joan, 50

safe houses, 53
satellite tracking, of sex offenders,
66–68
Schmidt, Stephanie, 66
Shakeshaft, Charol, 18–22
Shotwell, Kelley, 68
Sipes, Leonard A, 66
Smith v. Doe (2003), 9
Spencer, Elmer, Jr., 66
Standing Against Global
Exploitation (SAGE), 52
states
civil commitment laws in, 66–67
predator laws in, 56
satellite tracking of offenders by,
67–68
Steen, Charlene, 101, 102
Supreme Court
on involuntary commitment,
57–58, 67
on sex-offender registration, 8
surveys, on gay teachers, 87–88

teachers/school employees
homosexual, opinions on, 87–88
sexual misconduct among, 17
failure of Department of
Education to study, 19–20
by females, 98–99
lack of data on, 20–21
prevalence of, 18–19, 22
Tell, David, 69
terminology, of child sexual abuse,
88–89
Thorstad, David, 81

thought control, in treatment of
sexual predators, 62–63
Thrailkill, Charlotte Mae, 96, 98,
100–101, 102–103
Timmendequas, Jesse, 7
Titicut Follies (documentary), 60
Townsend, Kathleen Kennedy, 65
"Trust Betrayed, A" *(Education
Week)*, 21

U.S. Conference of Catholic
Bishops, 18, 23

victims
gender of, 78
and offender sexual orientation,
89–90
male, of female abusers, 99,
101–102
Village Voice (newspaper), 83
Violent Youth Predator Act
(proposed), 59

Washington Blade (newspaper), 83
Waters, Flint, 48
Weekly Standard (magazine), 83
Wilkinson, Peter, 104
Wolfe, Florence, 99
women
as child sexual abusers, 96–97
same-sex sexual experiences
among, 79

Yee, Leland, 52
Yockey, Joel Douglas Walton,
69–70, 76
Young, Allen, 80

Zonana, Howard V., 59